The Science of
SINGLE

The Science of
SINGLE

One Woman's Grand Experiment in Modern Dating,
Creating Chemistry, and Finding Love

Rachel Machacek

RIVERHEAD BOOKS

New York

RIVERHEAD BOOKS
Published by the Penguin Group
Penguin Group (USA) Inc.
375 Hudson Street, New York, New York 10014, USA
Penguin Group (Canada), 90 Eglinton Avenue East, Suite 700, Toronto, Ontario M4P 2Y3, Canada
(a division of Pearson Penguin Canada Inc.)
Penguin Books Ltd., 80 Strand, London WC2R 0RL, England
Penguin Group Ireland, 25 St. Stephen's Green, Dublin 2, Ireland (a division of Penguin Books Ltd.)
Penguin Group (Australia), 250 Camberwell Road, Camberwell, Victoria 3124, Australia
(a division of Pearson Australia Group Pty. Ltd.)
Penguin Books India Pvt. Ltd., 11 Community Centre, Panchsheel Park, New Delhi—110 017, India
Penguin Group (NZ), 67 Apollo Drive, Rosedale, North Shore 0632, New Zealand
(a division of Pearson New Zealand Ltd.)
Penguin Books (South Africa) (Pty.) Ltd., 24 Sturdee Avenue, Rosebank, Johannesburg 2196,
South Africa

Penguin Books Ltd., Registered Offices: 80 Strand, London WC2R 0RL, England

The publisher does not have any control over and does not assume any responsibility for author or third-party websites or their content.

First Riverhead trade paperback edition: January 2011

Library of Congress Cataloging-in-Publication Data

Machacek, Rachel.
The science of single : one woman's grand experiment in modern dating, creating chemistry, and finding love / Rachel Machacek.
p. cm.
ISBN 978-1-59448-496-4
1. Man-woman relationships. 2. Dating (Social customs) 3. Dating services-United States. 4. Machacek, Rachel. I. Title.
HQ801.M2339 2011
306.81'53092—dc22
[B]

2010017135

PRINTED IN THE UNITED STATES OF AMERICA

10 9 8 7 6 5 4 3 2 1

For my sister, Sarah

ACKNOWLEDGMENTS

Gratitude, peace and love to:

Mary Anna and John Machacek, my parents. My template for love is rooted in your endless afterwork hugs in the kitchen when I was little and the fact that you still hold hands, even after four decades together. I'm holding out for that kind of romance.

Michael McCarthy for being the kind of mentor and friend everyone should have at some point in her life.

Debra Leithauser for turning my half-baked, Merlot-ridden idea into a true assignment.

Bridget Wagner for having the brilliant idea for me to actually write a book about this, and making it happen.

Megan Lynch for calm guidance, and somehow (miraculously) prodding me into telling this story in less than six hundred pages.

The people who set me up with their friends, offered food and shelter when I traveled (and at home), put pen to paper and edited my drafts, rooted me on, and listened to me hash through every last detail as I made my way through this process, particularly: Ted Baker, Carey Burke,

Cathy Chung, Margaret Foster, Jennifer Giesler, Tracy Glanton, Jeanne Glunz, Group, Josh King, Joshua Kohn, Liz Kuvinka, Fran Lovaglio, Rosa Lovaglio, Edie Mann, Sarah Machacek, Kristi McKeag, Jennifer Niederberger, Pia and Chris Nierman, Gina Schaefer, Carolyn Shutler, Ashby Strassburger, Heather and Craig Stouffer, Kathleen Sutter, and Nancy TeSelle.

The Sagalyn Agency, Riverhead Books, and

All of my boyfriends. Even if you never heard from me again, I think of you often.

INTRODUCTION

I can trace the origins of this book back to one night—the night I went on a date with Mark, a man I'd met online.

There were omens that could have predicted that the evening, with a razor-sharp breeze in the dead of January, would end the way it did.

Omen #1: Mark was shirtless in one of his profile pictures. He had a hunky chest, but the fact that he needed to show it to the world right off the bat smacked of overcompensation.

Omen #2: On the way to our rendezvous point, I ran into a guy I'd broken up with in a heated email exchange a few months before. Actually, I saw the ex-whatever-he-was (what's the name for the emotionally unavailable guy you date for a few months but can never quite call your boyfriend?) coming toward me, pulled my wool cap low over my eyes, nipped my chin with the zipper on my puffer jacket, and feigned preoccupation with my cell phone so I wouldn't have to face him as he walked by not five feet away.

Omen #3: I was damaged goods. I forged into the bitter unknown and away from the harmony of my life, which includes a persistent orange cat called Bart and a studio apartment where I can survey my entire domain from every single corner and there are never any surprises. I was getting myself back out there after having my hopes of love and commitment shredded a few weeks before by yet another Ex-Whatever. He lived thousands of miles away, but had still managed to sequester a large percentage of my heart in the years we'd been friends. After four years of intermittent phone calls, somehow, I got the idea that maybe it would work out between us. I was almost relying on it, perhaps because even though there were just phone calls, he was the most consistent man in my life. My first and last visit to see him, which included a wretched night spent in hostel bunk beds, solidified the fact that it actually wasn't going to work out. You have to wonder about someone who's willing to haphazardly toss her love and commitment eggs into a single basket 3,000 miles away, like I did. I was a clueless romantic, and after this experience, I toughened up and decided I would only date men in my area code.

That's where Mark came in. Despite the omens, it should have been a perfect date. We met at L'Enfant, a small and dark café at the far end of Adams Morgan, the Washington, D.C., neighborhood where I live. It has exposed brick and the type of lighting that makes everyone's complexion glow, and it's a safe haven away from the short nightlife strip that's an odd conglomeration of hookah lounges, sports bars, and coffee shops.

Maybe it was first-date jitters, but Mark was a tough customer. Like a circus lackey, I jumped through hoops trying to get him to show a little teeth, or even curl up the corners of his mouth into a mere hint of a smile. And for two hours, I watched Mark's face vacillate between a sour-grapes grimace and a deer-in-headlights freeze. I worked through two drinks, a salad, and a bowl of soup, and by the end of it, he made it painfully clear that he did not like me or my sideshow. He expressed this without uttering a single word. Instead, he ceremoniously opened the bill and set it between us so we both could see—and pay.

I've found that not picking up the tab is a universal sign men use to express that there won't be a second date, though I was pretty sure Mark's email said, "Can *I* buy *you* a drink?" So I let him struggle over the math of who owed what, we each paid for exactly what we consumed, and left.

That bit at the café was the cakewalk, and it was the next ten minutes trudging home together that tested the boundaries of excruciating pain. Trying to get Mark to pull his conversational weight was like yanking wisdom teeth without an ounce of Novocain. By the time we reached my street corner, I'd expended all of my energy and felt as deflated as a four-day-old Mylar balloon. I'd tried with this man, and I'd failed. But people are people, and we're all trying to get by in this cold, harsh world, so I stopped to shake hands, hug, and offer a proper good-bye. Mark didn't stop. He picked up his pace into a trot, barely turning his head as his "Nice to meet you" was diced apart by the shards of ice blowing in the winter wind.

I'd been dealing with mostly passive rejection up until then, so this was a sharp, stinging slap across my already frostbitten cheek.

Men were now, quite literally, running away from me.

I walked myself to my own door, plopped down on my floor-model Ikea couch, and downed half a bottle of three-dollar merlot while Bart headbutted my cheek with his wet nose. Frustration, confusion, and anger that needed avenging coursed through my veins. They funneled up to my heart, and by the time the emotions reached my brain, they had mixed themselves into a productive email to an editor pitching a story about dating that turned into an article reviewing dating self-help books that turned into an idea to write a book about dating. Not a dating-advice book, though. An investigation—an *experiment*—to see what happens when you use all the resources you possibly can to meet and date the opposite sex.

I've always recognized dating as a necessary evil in life, even during my serial-monogamist phase back in high school and through my early twenties when I sashayed from one long-term relationship to the next, barely blinking an eye. I thank my mom for this wisdom. Just as my dad ingrained in me that a car's oil needs to be changed every three months or three thousand miles, she pounded into my head how important it is to see what and who's out there before committing to marriage—lest I settle for someone out of convenience, I suppose. The problem has always been that I've never thrived on meeting new people or making small talk with strangers, and this has made connecting with the opposite sex, let alone dating, about as compelling as getting a tetanus shot. So mostly, over the last seven years that I've been without a boyfriend, I'd taken to holing up in my apartment on Saturday nights, eating whole pans of chocolate chip cookies, never lifting a finger to find a date, and then complaining to my friends how there are no good guys left and how I hated dating. It's *so hard*, I'd say. But I didn't have a clue.

Despite my laissez-faire approach, I would land a date here and there. A friend of a friend, a man I'd met online when I'd finally conjured some moxie to try the Internet, or someone I dated way back when who squirmed his way back into the picture. I was probably averaging four dates a year, and one of those would inevitably turn into a half-baked relationship that ended at the two- or three-month mark and exactly when I started to want and expect more than the bread crumbs of emotion and intimacy that were being tossed at my feet.

So no, dating has never been my forte, though I don't think I'm a special case in this regard. I think it's tough for lots of people, judging from the conversations I've had with single men and women alike. Perhaps part of this reason is historical. In the United States, dating didn't exist until the Victorian era, when, for the first time, love became a prerequisite to marriage. (Prior to this, men based their marriage criteria on the fecundity of women, who could pop out kids to help on the farm. There's no reason to date and get to know someone if you're not worried about an actual emotional connection and are simply looking for free labor.) For the wealthy folks, a man showed a woman that he liked her by giving her his card, and if she gave him her card, it jump-started a stuffy courting ritual that took place at the girl's house, in the parlor, with parental supervision.

Lower- and middle-class families didn't have the proper home for this sort of thing, so couples met out in public. The rich kids soon followed suit because courting in public was considered "exciting." And here we have dating.

The process shifted with the Great Depression and then again during World War II, when dating was put on hold due to lack of funds or because men went off to battle. By the late 1940s, it was back to the formal rituals. Hand-scripted cards were traded in for pins and letter jackets, and couples married much younger (the median age for first marriages was, in 1950, 20.3 for women and 22.8 for men). People went steady with their future mates in high school, and if that didn't work out, there was always college.

Then came the Pill and women's liberation, and a woman needed a man like a fish needed a bicycle. Women embraced their choices and more and more weren't choosing marriage right away. Instead they pursued their career, uninterrupted by pregnancy and wedlock.

Since then, the median age for first marriages continues to rise (in 2007, it was 26 for women and 27.7 for men), and there now are more single people than ever—in fact, according to the 2006 Census Bureau report, there are 92 million single adults roaming the U.S. with nary a clue (or desire, in some cases) of how to change that. That's 42 percent of all U.S. residents. This makes me wonder why, if there are so many single people, it is so hard to find a date.

It's actually not, I discovered during this experiment—as long as you're putting yourself out there. It's a scary thing, though, being "out there." Menacing, in fact. I *like* my friends' homes in the suburbs, with their comfortable couches that have end tables where I can place my glass of merlot while watching a frothy movie about Hollywood love that always works out, no matter what. It's welcoming and cozy and I know what to expect. Being "out there" does not sound like this. It sounds more like walking into the middle of a treeless field with the singleton cross I've been bearing all these years, dead grass crunching under bare feet, and staking said cross in the barren terra firma. With the cross firmly planted, I climb up and tie myself to it, spread-eagle and not un-biblical-like. Soft spots are exposed and I'm defenseless against the prey that begin scary courting rituals and mating dances, similar to that of the Blue Wildebeest, which attracts its mate by rubbing its preorbital gland on a tree and then goring the tree with its horns.

Maybe other single people feel this way, too, and that's why they're not bothering to date anymore, which was the surprise discovery of the Pew Internet & American Life Project (hereafter the Pew Project), a 2005 survey of Internet users to see how online dating affected relationships in America. Researchers found that just 16 percent of singles said they're currently looking for a romantic partner—that's 7 percent of the adult population. More telling: 55 percent of singles reported no active interest in seeking a romantic partner and 36 percent hadn't been on a single date in three months. I had no idea I was in such good company.

Despite the Pew Project's bleak numbers over the single nation's "muted zest for romance," the dating and relationships market is booming. It doesn't take a bloodhound to sniff out the dollar signs. The National Singles Association reports that, based on U.S. Census Bureau numbers, the number of unmarried men and women in their early thirties has tripled in the last thirty years as a result of delaying marriage and changing societal norms, and that single adults make up half of all U.S. consumer units, frittering away an annual $1.6 trillion on shoes, MP3s, trips to Costa Rica, and cases of wine. As of 2009, the U.S. dating industry was a $1.8 billion business, according to "The U.S. Dating Services Market" report published by Marketdata Enterprises Inc., and there are thousands of resources everywhere for the people who *are* looking to date.

I should have been married and divorced twice and holding hands with fiancé number three by now, given all the options, but I've tried with all my might to avoid the hoopla of big-business profiteering on my single status. I'm a purist. I want to meet someone naturally, like in a continuing-education class, which is how my parents met, or thumbing through wilted spinach at the Safeway on Columbia Road. I also wouldn't mind if Mr. Right magically appeared at my doorstep, preferably on a golden day in April, with a bunch of pink peonies and Sam Cooke singing "You Were Made for Me" in the background.

But really, how do couples meet? The methods seem to have changed rather significantly in a short period of time. The 2005 Pew Project found that most couples met at work or school (38 percent), through family or friends (34 percent), or at a nightclub, bar, café, or other social gathering (13 percent). Only 3 percent reported meeting online and even fewer—1 percent—met on a blind date or through a dating service. However, as the Internet has taken over most areas of our lives, so too has it affected how we meet potential romantic partners.

A 2007 to 2009 Stanford University study (Meeting Online: The Rise of the Internet as a Social Intermediary) by associate professor of sociology Michael Rosenfeld, found that most couples surveyed, regardless of when they met, did so through friends (32 percent), which is in line with the Pew Project results. However, just under 30 percent of the couples who met in the two years preceding the survey met online. A 2010 Match.com survey conducted by the research firm Chadwick Martin Bailey discovered even higher numbers—one in five couples met online. And it's the people over thirty who are taking to cyberspace more than their twentysomething counterparts as it becomes increasingly more difficult to meet potential partners the further you get from school days; 51 percent of Match.com users are thirty to forty-nine years old, and the fifty-plus age group is their fastest-growing demographic.

These numbers and the overall shift in meeting people and dating explains quite nicely why I don't meet men on a regular basis, whether I'm shopping for spinach or driving thirty miles to my editing job at a magazine, where I'm surrounded by women and married men. I missed the shoo-in college-boyfriend-turned-husband love boat. Twice. I let the one who I thought was The One become The Ex. I seem to have exhausted my friends' single friends, and everyone knows it's impossible to meet anyone other than drunken guys at a bar—though my friends Craig and Heather met at a sweaty frat club in Georgetown, and I used to go there hoping that maybe I'd meet someone, too. All I found, though, was herds of scary wildebeests.

I'd done the best I could on my own, but with the trail of Ex-Whatevers clunking behind me like sand-filled milk cartons jerry-rigged to a chain slung around my ankles—a weighty reminder of exactly how many relationships haven't worked out— drastic measures were in order. I thought if I treated dating like an experiment where I was not only a participant but also an observer, I could discover a better way to date.

I should say right now that I'm no scientist. I don't have a degree in psychology, sociology, or chemistry, and words like *methodology* and *structure* make my ears bleed from the inside out. The last science experiment I worked on was in seventh grade when I hypothesized the effects of music on plant growth. I tested for three days and came to the astonishing conclusion that the *1812 Overture* is like steroids for green things. So, I lied. Sorry, Ms. Leskovar. Nonetheless, I will apply basic scientific methodology to my plan.

MY NOT-SO SCIENTIFIC METHOD

Question: What happens when you use all the resources you possibly can to meet the opposite sex? Are chemistry and love inevitable?

Hypothesis: I'll be out there. I'll meet people. Men. Lots of men. I'll get better at dating. I'll spend lots of money. But I won't meet anyone special. (Not to be a downer here. I'm just going with my track record.)

Approach: Meet men online, attend singles events, let the pros and friends set me up, read self-help books, see what dating is like in other cities, and sign up with a dating coach so I can learn to meet men on my own. The idea was to spend a month in each realm, during which time I'd date three or four guys.

Oh, the best laid plans . . .

I tried to keep the experiment as authentic as possible and, for the most part, only went out with men I was truly interested in. I didn't tell most of my dates about the experiment, with the exception of three blind dates and the men I went out with in other cities. (It was too tricky to keep up with a lie about why I was asking to go out with someone thousands of miles away.) To protect innocent and unwitting participants, I've used aliases and changed minor details.

The concern everyone seemed to have when I started this experiment was "What if you meet someone?" My original reply: "I haven't met anyone in seven years. Why would I now?" Then my mom pointed out that anyone who truly understands me, cares about me, and is worth my time would understand. And as bitter as I can be at times, I firmly believe that if it's meant to work out, it will.

Here's what happened. (I'll start from the beginning.)

Online Dating

A Lesson in Keeping Great Expectations in Check

There he is, leaning against a pergola, on the rooftop deck at the Reef, awkwardly looking down at his cell phone as you do when you're waiting by yourself at a bar for someone you met online. He must be hoping to high heaven that:

1. I'm not crazy,

2. I posted reliable pictures that were
   a. of me and
   b. not taken before I gained 100 pounds, and

3. I show up.

Scrappy13 (that's his handle) and I met on Match.com, which, along with the Onion Personals, I'd been browsing for a few weeks. You can become a member of both sites for free, but once you want to start contacting other members, you have to pay. Generally, it's about thirty-five dollars for a one-month package, but if you buy in bulk, the monthly fee goes down significantly.

I'd been lying low in the virtual brush, patiently waiting out my first conquest. More hiding than waiting, actually. Even though I'd dated online before, I was skittish about going back into the jungle. The most recent guy I dated broke it off with me because it "wasn't fun anymore," which was true. But who wants to hear that? He might as well have told me I looked fat in every single pair of jeans I owned.

The current prospects, while entertaining, were not at all endearing. I'd received emails from men on both sites that went exactly like this, typos, craziness and all:

Hello Pretty, is my pleasure to know you and to love you as my arm length, looking through your pic at match.com, i can see the love in your eyes. Am from Nigeria, Lagos city 25yrs and I will want you and i to get really close if you don't mine were my country is. As the star is far from the moon they love each other and they will want to try and know each other no matter what will want to distract them. i really want to have you and to love cos you make me felt that thelove must come from you, in other for you to contact me this is my email . . .

and

Younger 20s guy is HOT!

and

You look like trouble

Scrappy13 was harmless enough—a thirty-five-year-old who, in his profile, discussed properly executing "the most revered of dance moves (the Lawnmower)," referred to his family as a modern-day Brady Bunch, and in general seemed like a fully functioning member of society. And he could spell, which I personally appreciate as much as I appreciate good shoes. (You can tell a lot about a man by his shoes.) He winked at me—there's a winking emoticon you can click in lieu of sending an email—and, after a week of epic emails, here we are. He doesn't look like the *best* picture from his profile, but at least I recognize him. He is pale, freckly, and wearing square-toed shoes.

It's just a date. It's just a date. It's just a date.

I'm strategically a few minutes late because I hate being the one waiting, looking up at every single person walking by and wondering, "Is that him?" and "Maybe that guy?" As I approach Scrappy13, sweaty from nerves and the three-story climb up to the deck, I feel my smile descend into a constipated grimace. I've learned to fake extraversion, but in situations like first dates where I have no control and can't predict the outcome, I'm grabbing for the panic button at the first hello.

On top of this, I engage in ridiculous expectation-building when it comes to dating because, ultimately, I do want to get married, have kids, and scream bloody murder at the whole family that they *will* wash their hands before we sit down to dinner, whilst wielding a spatula dripping with spaghetti sauce. Dating is the conduit to this, so it's almost counterintuitive not to go in with the endgame in mind. I can't tell you how many times I've thought to myself in the mirror when applying a last coat of lip gloss, "This might be the night I meet The One!" I build in an impossible standard with my fantasizing. I'll visualize a wedding dress—maybe even the flower arrangements—before I even get to the date.

Scrappy13 doesn't know about my dating neuroses, so he shakes my clammy hand instead of leaping off the edge of the roof deck. As I'd suspected, he's shorter than me, even though his shoes easily add an extra inch. I knew this because every single guy I've ever met online who's said he's somewhere between five foot eight and five foot eleven has been two inches shorter. Studies at the University of Chicago and MIT back this up. Researchers found that when dating online, men do lie about height—though only by an inch. They also lie about how educated they are and marital status, while women fudge their weight by shaving off at least ten pounds and lie about their overall physical appearance. And everyone lies about age.

The height issue is my thing, though it probably doesn't even register on the brain of the average woman who is five foot four. I, however, am four and a half inches taller than that, and those crummy few inches are the difference between expectations met and a deal breaker. This begs the question of why I need to date someone who is taller than I am. I don't. And I haven't always. But there's something about not wanting to feel like an Amazon. But I can't cast stones at Scrappy13 though, since I labeled my body type as "slender" rather than the more accurate "about average." In the spirit of even Steven, I take my height grievances that run deep and heavy through my being and put them off to the side where I can still see them, but so they're not clouding my judgment.

Bon Jovi blares directly over our table while Scrappy13 and I tiptoe through the getting-to-know-you process and I silently contemplate if I think he's cute. With online dating, if you're looking at a screen full of blah guys, the mediocre guy will shine like Adonis in comparison. I wasn't sure how I felt about him when he winked at me, so I'd called in for a second opinion, which helps temper my propensity for bad decision making fueled by desperation. My reinforcements are coworkers Edie and Donna. They're my age, smart, and married. Both escaped from small, rural towns where people talk with accents you'd need pliers to pull apart, and this is why I trust their judgment; they've seen all kinds and can tell me when I'm being rightfully choosy or just snotty.

"Oooooh, I *like* him." Edie leaned over my chair looking at my monitor.

Donna was right behind her. "He's *totally* cute."

Their double positive sealed the deal.

My in-person conclusion right now: He's not *not* cute. It's superficial, but that's how dating is. If you don't want to tear the clothes off the person you're on a date with, buttons flying everywhere, and jump into bed with them, what's the point? If attraction and sex weren't an issue, I'd never date; instead, I'd have lots of good friends and hug them a lot, and life would be easier and neater and uncomplicated.

"Sooooo . . . what do you do?" People love talking about their jobs here in D.C. It's a place where people come to get ahead by doing things like saving the world or taking over the world or writing press releases about saving and taking over the world. They define themselves by their work, which is not my thing. But I have to say *something*. Scrappy13 and I didn't connect at first meet, so I was digging for some commonality and the chemistry we found over email. I've dated online long enough to know that cyber sparks are unreliable when it comes to predicting in-person sparks, and I shouldn't be surprised that ours is stuck in my Gmail account, password protected and not going to make a showing.

The career question has the desired effect of getting us into more of a conversation rather than interrogating each other. But immediately following a debriefing of his top-secret job that has something to do with creating weaponry (I only hear a fraction of it above Axl Rose's growl, which is a good thing, because talk of guns and missiles definitely isn't making him more attractive to my bleeding-heart liberalism), like a swift hit to the temple with a blunt object, our conversation falls into the first lull.

Music fills up every molecule of space on the roof deck, but the silence between us is suffocating. I don't know what disaster I think might happen during this unscheduled break in programming. In actuality, conversational lulls rarely last more than ten seconds (I made that number up), which is enough time to sip a beer, refold your napkin over your lap, or reach for your cell phone to make sure that it's off to prove how polite and conscientious you are on dates. But on a first date, ten seconds can feel like an eternity. Babies are born and people will die in those few breaths.

Instead of patiently waiting for natural conversation to pick up, the fight-or-flight response kicks in. I have to interject something. I launch into survival mode and start spouting off irrelevant information about my life, something I read or heard, but nothing with a punch line or any point whatsoever. I punctuate this nonsense with guffaws and too-quick, too-loud laughter, and descend quickly and without an ounce of grace into the damning fires of first-date hell.

And then the waiter with the diamond earrings that sparkle in the setting sun rescues me from myself. "You guys gonna get dinner?" The frenzy dies as quickly as it began, and I'm quiet.

"Should we get our dinner on?" Scrappy13 looks at me. I'm surprised he wants to continue this date. Maybe it's not as bad as I think it is. I've had enough to drink to agree, and I mostly keep my anxiety in check as we spend the next hour nervously laughing over interim "huhs?" and "can you repeat thats?" while I jump and skip through topics like a ten-year-old with ADD.

Standing outside on the sidewalk, Scrappy13 and I do the post-date shuffle.[1] Kissing isn't an option, and I'd been mulling over

---

[1] Typically done standing a couple feet away from each other, while the imperceptible shifting of feet magically turns the configuration at least 180 degrees. The less I like someone, the more I turn, presumably in an effort to ward off physical contact.

whether I even wanted to go out with him again, thinking probably not. I have a knack for getting myself trapped in relationships I'm too afraid to leave for fear of hurting the other person. Instead of breaking up because that's what people do when they don't want to date someone anymore, I convince myself that I need to try harder to make things work. There are three years of my life I'd like back based on this frustrating logic of pounding square pegs into round holes, and I now run with the idea that it's best to nip things in the bud early on.

"Do you want to go out again?"

Curses! Couldn't he have waited to discuss this over email so it would be easier for me to say no? The spotlight flashes on me and I'm naked in front of a packed house waiting for me to perform the turn-him-down-gently tango. Unlike the subtle postdate shuffle, I haven't practiced this dance. I don't know how to say no. Not like this. Not in person. I don't want to hurt Scrappy13's feelings, although it's vain of me to think he would care at all if I didn't want to see him again after only one date.

I hear the firm voice of my therapist, Judith, in my head, her nasal New York accent instructing me with well-placed questions. "Do you really think you can know if you like someone after one date?" she asks.

"Yes!" I yell back in my head, indignant. Presumably, people aren't always themselves on first dates and it's hard to gauge chemistry. I don't totally buy in to this, but I also know my one-strike-you're-out method hasn't worked. And I'm not good at listening to my gut anyway. I have no confidence in it. What if I'm confusing a gut reaction that's instinctually telling me I shouldn't date this person with a knee-jerk reaction to the fear of getting involved with someone? Or maybe I know this really can't go anywhere because I have many, many more dates to go on for this experiment, so my subconscious is making me less attracted to him.

I peer at Scrappy13 through the foggy lens of overanalysis. My heart is clenched into a "no" and my head is piercing with "just go." What if Judith is right? What if I say no and miss out on a good thing? And besides, what could one more date hurt?

"Sure!" I use "sure" instead of "yes." It means, "I will, but I don't really want to." I have much to work on in therapy.

"So, hooker, how did it go? Did you have sex?"

I'm postdate recapping over merlot and *The Golden Girls* with my neighbor Kenneth, who is equal parts crotchety old man and charming queen, and who gets great pleasure in calling me and anyone else who allows him to get away with it "hooker."

I met Kenneth the first day he moved into my building three years ago with his yippy Italian greyhound, Mick. He came barging up to our dilapidated roof deck while I was having a civilized summer date of chardonnay and cantaloupe with a guy I met online who I was certain was gay, despite his constant sex talk.

Kenneth was upset because he couldn't find our apartment manager's office to get the key to his top lock. "Honey, I don't know this neighborhood. I'm a Dupont girl," he said, referring to his old neighborhood Dupont Circle and fanning at the heat.

Since then we've become close friends, and he's one of my

only neighbors now because our building management company stopped renting out apartments a year ago, presumably in an attempt to empty out the building and convert to condo. We were the holdouts and we weren't leaving.

"Noooooo, we didn't have sex. It was a first date."

"Well, does he have a big penis?"

This may seem like a ridiculous question after having told him there wasn't any sex. But then you have to consider the gay dating sites manhunt.net and spandexguys.com, where penis size is a basic stat and there will probably be a picture of it, too.

"Well, he is short, so . . . tough to say." I play along for fun.

"When are you going to get over the height thing?" Kenneth doesn't approve of my hang-up. He thinks I don't give people a chance. Which is true. But this also is coming from someone whose friends are mostly thin and pretty. We all have our criteria, and usually it's pretty shallow.

Spinning your wheels does not create chemistry.

Over the next week, I roll up my sleeves and plow through single-ton cyberspace.[2] I check my accounts wherever there's an open

---

[2] It is necessary to differentiate dating sites for singles since there are also online dating sites for married people, specifically The Ashley Madison Agency. It sounds like a brothel and their tagline is: "Life is short. Have an affair." They even have an affair-guarantee program. Gracious.

Internet connection: during my lunch break, every five minutes for the rest of the day, and into the wee hours on my couch in my underwear, laptop burning my thighs.

In the midst of a G-rated cyber affair with Scrappy13 that includes epic emails all day long but not a single phone call, another guy on Match, TheKid, winks at me. I seem to be getting a better response on this site, probably because there are more members here than the Onion, which, along with other online magazines including Nerve.com and Salon.com, uses the FastCupid.com database. It's a niche site hyped as the "eclectic online community for people who already have a life!" Whatever that means. More precisely, Match, with more than 20 million members (according to the website), is like a giant party at a club with all the frat boys, whereas the Onion (with 256,000 members) is like going to an intimate dinner party with intellectuals. The guests might be better, but that dinner party is small, so pickings are slim.[3] I want to be at the party where there's more bang for the buck.

TheKid is twenty-six. He's too young, but he's *really* excited

[3] Online dating sites count "active members" as anyone who has a profile posted, has logged in during the past year, and has an active email address. Active members aren't necessarily paying customers, and if customers aren't paying, they cannot respond to emails you or I might send to them. In other words, the number of profiles that show up on a page is not entirely indicative of how many members are actually currently using the dating site. The best way to know if someone is active is to see when they last logged on, which is usually listed on the member's profile page. I always steer clear of members who haven't logged on in more than three months.

about me. Actually, he's excited about everything. His profile is overflowing with emoticons and exclamation points. And then there are the misspellings. It's so hard not to be judgmental when it comes to spelling. As an editor, it gives me distinct pleasure to find typos just about anywhere. In a sense, that would make this a perfect match. But no one ever wants to see a typo on a resume or cover letter, and that's what we're talking about here.

These aren't misspellings from typing too fast, either. These are words like "excersice" that he butchers repeatedly because he thinks he knows how they're spelled. But the last book he read was *The Grapes of Wrath*, and he's a teacher. With a master's degree. (This fact did conjure a snotty internal monologue about how *anyone* can get a master's these days.) His favorite things are "Sushi, Traveling, Excersice, Sweating, Love." Hmmmm. So I don't connect with what he's saying or how he's saying it—at all—but he's terribly cute. And he wants to meet someone who's "outgoing, caring, energetic, and intelligent. She also must have a great sense of humor and like to laugh a lot. Enjoying life is also a plus ;)." I like life. I'm caring and intelligent. So I email him.

Like his profile, TheKid's emails explode with alpha-numeric excitability. I wonder if maybe he "excersices" too much. Serotonin appears to be shooting out of his fingertips, through the keyboard, and into my apartment. I decide this is a good thing. I'm generally a happy person—with the help of antidepressants, that is—so there's something to be said for surrounding myself with happy people.

TheKid's emails are warm and friendly, and when I tell him it's my birthday that weekend, he "sings" to me in all caps with twelve exclamation points and three smiley faces. It's also Memorial Day weekend and he is going out of town. We make a date for the following Sunday, and I go to my family birthday dinner where I receive two cards each from my mom, dad, and sister (and one from the cat), and my mom winces as if red ants were crawling up her legs because there are no candles to blow out on my apple cobbler. The whole biological-clock-ticking business has escaped me thus far, but I think my mom is dying for some grandkids who will truly appreciate the pomp and circumstance that goes along with our familial celebrations. Bart will only tide her over for so long.

I turned thirty-three and had the feeling it would be a special year. I'd been looking forward to it ever since I read an interview on Pitchfork.com with Billy Corgan, who revealed how his early nineties angst subsided after his Saturn Return phase—aka the "early life crisis," which usually strikes in the late twenties. This period in my own life was darkened with depression because I was accustomed to coasting along and I had no idea what I wanted to do or who I wanted to be. So I took off. I moved to New York for a year, then to an island for a summer, where I lived in a tent and worked in a hut, and finally traveled around Europe because I'd always wanted to. I was searching and escaping at the same time. When I ran out of money and couldn't justify another expense on my credit card, I moved back to D.C. and hunkered down at my parents' house, sleeping in my old bedroom for a year and a half while I figured out my life.

I'd spent the last few years stabilizing my existence and my debt, I'd lost the weight I'd gained while trying to fill the vacant hole of my existence with an Oreo cookie prescription, and I was lighter emotionally than I'd ever been. I wanted to celebrate because I was convinced that, by now, the residual effects of that tumultuous time would have dissipated. That was mostly true. Though by embarking on this experiment, I had unwittingly affected change in my life yet again.

The honeymoon is over. The initial rush of email you get from being fresh meat online has faded. I welcome the silence though, because I can only juggle so many dates and men at once, and after two weeks of fielding emails from guys I didn't want to go out with and vacillating between TheKid and Scrappy13, I was already burning out.

I tried to date two people simultaneously many years ago. It wasn't disastrous, but it also wasn't advisable, mostly because the guys were friends. We were all out at a bar one night, one boyfriend on the main level, the other upstairs. And me running up and down between the two trying to keep them separate. I promised one a date the next weekend, went home with the other, and ditched them both to get back together with The Ex. Then and now, I've found that when you're wrapped up in the process of dating and want so badly to have something work out with someone—anyone—it's easy to forget that your choices aren't limited to one person or the other. There's also the choice I always forget about: To not choose anyone in order to keep myself open to someone who *is* right for me.

I've let things with Scrappy13 cool. I suspect he understands that I'm uncertain. Or maybe he thinks I'm busy, because that's what I keep telling him. I've been more interested in getting to know TheKid, whom I'm more attracted to but have nothing in common with. Our first date was coffee in the park. I decided that, despite some juvenile tendencies (grasping at fireflies, hugging his new Honda Element), it was worth another more formal date. Our second rendezvous was meant to be a grown-up dinner date but felt more like a mom and her son because I'm so much older than him, because I felt like I had to handhold him to plan the date, and because, despite my shameless, wine induced puckering in the passenger seat when he dropped me off, all I got was a hug. "I'll call you," he said.

Afterward, I'd barged into Kenneth's apartment for a nightcap and another recap.

"So, how tall is he?"

"Barely my height." I plop down on his couch and hold my glass of wine over my head so it doesn't spill while Mick jumps up and down on my bladder like he's on a trampoline.

"He said he's five foot ten, but he's not. I know he's not." I slug down the wine and look at Kenneth sideways. "What's wrong with you people? Do you really not know how tall you are?"

Kenneth, with all of the smugness of a queen, cocks his head back at me and asks, "Have you ever thought *you*, hooker, are the one who's wrong?"

Well. No. I've measured myself a half million times and always come back with the same five feet, eight and a half inches. But maybe, just maybe, I'd grown. I'd been going to a chiropractor for a year, after all. Maybe I've been stretched out an inch—or even two.

Determined to crack the height mystery once and for all, I march across the hall to my apartment and fumble through the everything drawer that's jammed with kitchen utensils, batteries, talking bottle openers, miniature flashlights, and all other miscellany that doesn't fit anywhere else, looking for a tape measure. I wind up with seamstress tape, the loosey-goosey kind that you can wrap around your hips and waist; not exactly the best tool for an accurate vertical reading, especially when one has been drinking. I stand against the inside of the archway in my living area looking into my full-length mirror fifteen feet away while aiming a pen at the wall above my head. I come out with almost five foot ten. I make another green squiggly line and measure again. Five foot nine. Another attempt: five feet, nine and a half inches. Despite the variance, it appears that, in fact, I *did* grow. I immediately update my dating profiles to reflect my new stature to five feet, ten inches. The riddle of the sphinx—solved.

My phone beeps five minutes later.

You grew?

It's a text from TheKid.

I'm alone in my apartment except for Bart, who's spread-eagle on the back of the green armchair, quietly attending to his balls, but my ears burn red anyway. I ignore the text. The next morning, an email awaits me from TheKid:

You grew?

This is followed up by a phone call that afternoon. "I've never known anyone that grew overnight."

"Well, you said you're five foot ten, but we seemed to be the same height, so I measured because I've been going to a chiropractor. It seems as though I have grown." I sound like an idiot.

He laughs. "I *thought* it was weird that we seemed to be the same height . . ."

Later that day, I measured myself again, this time with a sober line and real tape measure. I didn't grow. I was still the same old five feet, eight and a half inches I've always been, though I decided to round up to five foot nine, because apparently, that's what you do.

Caution in the wind has a nasty backhand.

Into week five of the experiment, there was a flurry of texts and emails with TheKid and Scrappy13 and I warmed again. Additionally, I was prepping for Tuesday drinks with CarrotTop, who winked at me over the Onion the week before. He's a writer, thirty-nine, six foot three, and says the last great book he read was *Forever* by Judy Blume.

I didn't get in touch with CarrotTop at first because I couldn't tell what he looked like in his profile picture. In his close-up, he wore sunglasses so I could only account for straight teeth. His other pictures reminded me of Carrot Top the comedian before aliens abducted him and replaced him with a plasticized clone. I spent a good thirty minutes clicking on CarrotTop's pictures, trying to decide what I thought. Ultimately, I decided to do nothing. I liked his profile, but I couldn't tell what he looked like. I looked at his pictures again the next day, presumably under the impression that I'd developed superhuman vision overnight that would have allowed me to *really* see what he looked like behind his shades. Of course, I couldn't, and so decided that, like the profiles of guys with no shirts on and profiles without pictures (PWPs), profiles with pictures of guys wearing sunglasses are no-nos. Too many unknowns.

But CarrotTop saw that I was stalking his profile through the "Who's Viewing Me" link, which lets you see everyone who has checked you out, and he sent an email.

We should talk already!

Oh, okay. We volleyed funny emails and made a drink date. How bad could it be? If nothing else, he's tall.

I've had plenty of women tell me that they ended up marrying someone they never thought they'd be attracted to. He was so funny, or so caring, or had a personality so superlative that it made up for bald spots, hairy backs, and bad teeth. Once I saw Carrot-Top, though, I wanted to duck under the bar or sidle out the back door. He didn't look like I thought he would look. It wasn't his face that gave me pause. It was those damn sunglasses—the ones that got me into this mess—dangling from disintegrating Croakies; it was the crumpled black tee clearly swiped out from under a pile of wet towels in haste and tucked into the checkered pants that made him look like he should be darting around in a clown-car routine.

Based on his stylistic blunders, I'd conjured a vision of Carrot-Top's apartment: a mass of dirty clothes strewn over the bed and chairs, half-empty coffee mugs with floating mold, and a tangy, unidentifiable smell. It was quite possible that CarrotTop had an immaculate, bacteria-free, sensibly furnished place. But first impressions are everything and, hell, I had spent some time applying mascara and coiffing my hair for him. But then, Judith's calm and cool voice of reason that lingers in my frontal lobe instructed me yet again to overlook the superficial crap. "Those things can be changed," it reminded me. Croakies can be burned, shirts washed and ironed, pants tailored so they're not high-waters. So I didn't run, and instead focused on the positive: Finally, someone had exceeded the height requirement.

"Should we get mojitos?" CarrotTop pronounces it *mo-jee-toes*, and with this suggestion, an epic three-hour date at Meze, a little Mediterranean joint down the street, ensued.

CarrotTop has been talking nonstop since we sat down at our table on the patio. We got a sweet spot right on the corner by the sidewalk that would have been a lot sweeter if the adjacent table hadn't been inches away and occupied by a couple who'd been eavesdropping on our conversation. They shot me looks of sympathy as CarrotTop made it evident to everyone within a six-foot radius that this is our first date and, yes, we met online. "Look at me, look at me," he seemed to shout without even opening his mouth.

Despite the tsunami of craziness around him, I don't think I'd ever met someone that comfortable in his own skin, and I found that endearing. Unfortunately, he lacked any sense of subtlety.

"What kind of mojito are you getting?" I go for an obvious conversational opener even though with CarrotTop, I don't need to say a word.

"Eh?" He puts his finger to his right ear.

"What kind . . . ?" I point to the menu.

"Oh. Sorry. I don't hear so good. You're gonna hafta speak up."

He's not kidding. He played in a band for years. A lot of loud music he said.

Adrenaline whistles straight out of each and every hair follicle in my head. I don't know if I can do this. I can't spout off my life details in a voice that will inevitably engage the two-top next to us, the four-top at our diagonal, and anyone hustling by on the sidewalk. So I make like a clam, which CarrotTop gleefully takes as his cue. He swaggers onto center stage and launches into his comedy routine. (He did say in his profile that he wanted to try stand-up, which I took to be a positive because I adore funny men. I certainly didn't realize he meant that he wanted to do this on a date.)

It's not long before he starts unself-consciously and quite purposefully dropping words like "retard" and "homo." He has definitely crossed the border from off-color into inappropriate, and that, even for someone like me, who thinks political correctness could stand a good flogging, is deal-breaker territory.

My only escape is my drink, so I drink more. So does Carrot-Top, and he gets louder and more absurd. We move from short buses to his tooth retainer, which he shows me by flinging his head back and pointing to the metal contraption binding the back of his two front teeth. "Hee . . . ere it eh. Haight ere." I don't seem interested enough so he flings his head back again. The date has become a series of dirty bombs going off every minute like clockwork, yet somehow, instead of running for cover, I stay and absorb every last piece of shrapnel flung my way. I blame the mojeetos. They made me dumb and hungry, and so I say yes to ordering food.

Just as the hummus and pita is set between us, Jeannine walks by. Jeannine is my soul mate. I met her a couple years ago; I was quitting my part-time job working at a hardware store and she was starting. Since then, we've dissected every morsel of the male psyche on one couch or another while drinking enormous bottles of chardonnay.

"Hey!" I grab her arm and practically rip it off, I'm so relieved to see her. I introduce her to CarrotTop. She's smiling a little too widely. I know what she's thinking: *What the fuck?* I know what CarrotTop is thinking, too: *More audience!* I can hear the jackpot bell going off in his head.

"I love Rachel's hair. Isn't it pretty?" CarrotTop endears himself to Jeannine with compliments to her friend.

I am indeed having a fabulous hair day, which are few and far between when you're in the perpetual grow-out stage I linger in.

"Why, yes, it is." Jeannine cocks her head to the side, bemused, while I smile off into space pretending that this is the most normal date ever. I want Jeannine to whisk me away, but I know that isn't a possibility, so I'm thankful when she leaves because I can't take the whole business of worlds colliding. I don't want Carrot-Top infringing on my inner circle. Ever.

"I have to go to the little boy's room. I'll understand if you're not here when I get back." CarrotTop hops up from his chair. Jesus. Seriously. Save me. Someone. Save me. I sit motionless while he's gone, allowing the atoms that have been whipping around my head to settle down so I can think clearly. And just as I gather together my discombobulated senses . . .

"You're still here!"

He's back.

At one point, I did seriously consider hopping the rail and booking it home, though I don't think I could ever tap into the cowardice it would take to ditch a date.

"Of course I am!"

I suck down the last of mojito number two, and since the hummus is mostly gone, I'm thinking (hoping) this is the end. Then, our waiter drops off a third round. When did we order those? He sets down CarrotTop's pineapple mojito, leans over him to deliver mine, and exits stage left.

CarrotTop leans over the table and whispers. "Did you smell his armpits?"

"Uh, nooooo." I brace myself.

"Well." He leans in closer with a dramatic pause. "I'm probably going to get in trouble for saying this, but . . ." He pauses again and slowly glances left, then right. ". . . his armpits . . ." Looks down to pause. ". . . they smelled like . . ." He leans in, cupping his right hand around his mouth, voice lowered to an exaggerated whisper. ". . . *vagina*." He enunciates the word carefully and through his nasal passage so that the *gine* syllable makes my arm hair stand up and shake.

I'm speechless. But then I lean back in my plastic deck chair and smile with the same satisfaction Bart has after he's finally broken me down and I get up at 5 a.m. to feed him.

"What?"

The tables have turned. I've caught CarrotTop off guard.

"Ohhhh, nothing. It's just that my coworkers will thank you tomorrow for this story."

"Really? I've made it into your water cooler talk?"

Oh, you have no idea. "Definitely!" We both laugh, though I'm pretty sure for different reasons.

CarrotTop's follow-up email comes a couple days later:

> How funny was it that on our first date I said the server smelled like a vagina? I'd love to go out again.

I wait two days to write back, agreeing that the vagina comment was indeed priceless but that I wasn't feeling it. I never thought I'd be pairing those thoughts together.

On Wednesday, I'm hanging out in Kenneth's apartment and surfing for men on his laptop because my Internet connection is spotty.

"Can't you do that in your own apartment?" Kenneth is annoyed, and he should be because I'd walked in without knocking, plopped on his couch, and picked up his laptop.

"No. My Internet sucks." He doesn't fight it and goes back to CNN while I click and scroll and click again on Match, cruising by mug shot after mug shot. I pause on Dr.Dreamy, a boyish-looking thirty-nine-year-old internist with dark wavy hair. He's five foot ten (so he says), vegetarian, Libra, likes using parentheses (me too!), and is interested in *someone who's natural* (me), *creative* (me), *liberal, easygoing, fun* (me, me, me!). I almost don't email him because I'm not sure I can take the rejection from someone so perfect.

"Do you think he's cute?" I turn the laptop around so Kenneth can see.

"Ooooh. Yes! Love the hair."

I bashfully wink at Dr.Dreamy, which is ridiculous because according to a study called "What Makes You Click: An Empirical Analysis of Online Dating," 70 percent of women can expect a response from men when they take the initiative and send out the first email.

He emails me the next morning. Yay! He's receptive and funny and we set up a date for the following Tuesday because I've over-booked myself with plans to go out with Scrappy13 on Friday night and TheKid on Saturday afternoon. The back-to-back dates seemed like a good idea. I could get them out of the way to have more time for friends because over the last four weeks I'd canceled on my book club, craft night, and random weekend nights out, and the only time left between looking for dates, dating, and work seemed to be for sleeping.

When I finally do make it out of the house on Thursday night to go to Pharmacy Bar, a grungy dive for hipsters who like to play

Buck Hunter and smoke American Spirits, my newish friend Jen asks what I've been up to. When I tell her about all the dates, she laughs and tells me she thought I was never around because I didn't like hanging out with them. It would have been an abrupt comment from anyone else. But she gets away with it for the same reason she gets away with wearing a blue vest over short shorts with high-heeled fringe boots while drinking Elijah Craig Single Barrel: she gets away with everything.

"No way. I've been so busy with this experiment. Finding dates, dating . . ."

"You girls need another drink?" Her boyfriend, Gabe, stands up from our booth and points at us. Gabe is only twenty-five but I always feel like he's at least eight years older than me. He's always taking care of everything and making sure everyone's okay.

I shake my beer bottle, which is half full.

"Nah."

"Cool. How about you, my dear?" He puts his hand on Jen's head, realizes she has a full glass of whiskey, and thinks better of it. "You're fine."

"Hey!" She's mock offended but shrugs her shoulders while taking another sip.

I look at her and giggle. She knows she's lucky to have Gabe. And for me, it's comforting to see that there are some good guys out there while I'm caught in a melee of not-quite-rights.

Massive Attack serenades Scrappy13 and me while we kiss in his car. I'm tipsy from a night of dinner, bowling, and more drinking.

It's the end of our fourth date, which started out almost contentious over tapas and sangria at Jaleo, a Spanish restaurant in Chinatown. Scrappy13 started quizzing me on guys I mentioned in passing, insinuating every male name I uttered was someone I'd been on a date with. Things had smoothed over at the bowling alley, where chemistry actually made a showing even though it seemed to hatch directly from the empty beer bottles in front of us.

Now, I get the feeling he's looking for the invite upstairs, but I have no intention of leaving first base or him leaving his car. When it's 2:30 a.m. and two drunk people are in a studio apartment and have to make a decision between a couch and the bed three feet away, there's no way not to send mixed signals.

At the same time, at this point in our relationship, I feel like I should want him to come upstairs. (The signs that I don't like him have turned into an aggressive picket line and are becoming impossible to ignore.) He's a good kisser, but the chemistry has waned at exactly the same rate that my buzz has worn off. It's gone by the time he goes for the boob grab, awkwardly reaching under my seat belt that's still fastened. There's a time and place for boob grabbing, and when you are thirty-five years old, you should know when and where that is. I gently push his hand aside, and pull back.

"I should probably go."

Back in my apartment, after practically stomping on Bart to keep him from escaping out the door, I have a silly drunken urge to throw Scrappy13 a bone. I send a text message to say good night (again) and that he's a really good kisser.

He texts back, presumably while driving because there's no way he's home yet.

> Scrappy13: Then why put an end to a good evening?
> Me: It's what feels right. I hope that's okay.

These are the things that should be talked about in person.

> How was the rest of your weekend. Friday was really fun! : P

Scrappy13 emails first thing Monday morning. I hadn't heard a peep from him all weekend. Usually, he would have texted me a few times and I couldn't help but feel a sense of relief that he hadn't, because ten hours after the boob grab, there was a hungover lunch date with TheKid that consisted of take-out crab cakes from the fish market and watching the World Cup, with me sunk into one side of his couch and he on the other. It was all very sixth grade.

Right after the date, which didn't end in a kiss even though I puckered up all over again when he dropped me off, I trucked over to the other side of town to get coffee with my friend Anna, who was in D.C. for the weekend. Then I dragged myself out to meet up with Jeannine, Jen, and Gabe at the Black Cat, because now I'm paranoid that my busy dating schedule has made them think I'm aloof when I'm really just tired.

Being sandwiched in a booth with my elbows sticking to the layer of sludge on the table and smoke seeping into my pores was fun for about ten minutes, until I realized I had nothing to talk about except the experiment and my dates. But everyone listens intently to my story about CarrotTop and they call me a "man-eater." It's embarrassing because I'm not, and I actually feel like this process is starting a slow chomp on my psyche. But I'm also secretly pleased that at least I give off the air of someone who knows what she's doing.

But I don't, and Scrappy13's email is confusing. I mean, yeah, we did have fun. But seriously. Huh? There was the text message in which he seemed to admonish me for ending the night.

I walk over to my editor's office looking for answers. Mike is a modern-day pied piper with an unflinching rosy glow and a horseshoe up his ass that makes you want to go along with him no matter what.

"Did I miss something here?" I sit on his office couch and prepare to be schooled.

He swivels around in his chair to face me and crosses his ankle on his knee. "No. Why wouldn't he want to keep dating you? You're a catch!"

"I don't think I want to go out with him though."

"Oh well. Don't."

He makes it sound so simple. "Yeah, but do I need to email him or should I call . . .?"

"Eh. Email him and tell him to go grab someone else's rack."

I laugh. "I'm serious. What's the protocol?"

Mike's been married for thirteen years and has three kids. I have no idea why I think he should have this answer. But he embraces the bigger-picture scripture of happiness that I so often overlook, and he seems to have the answers to everything else.

"Just email him. You don't owe him anything."

I get a second opinion. Edie agrees with Mike, and I send the let's-move-on email to Scrappy13 on Tuesday. Actually, I write the email and have Donna click send. When Scrappy13 responds, I call Edie over to read it before I can because I can't take a virtual snipe.

She leans over my desk to look at my monitor, laughs, and walks out the door, her husband's enormous Georgetown University sweatshirt swinging over her aerobicized ass. "You're fine."

It's not the "You're a bitch and thanks for leading me on" email I was expecting. Scrappy13 wasn't an asshole at all. His email was that of a well-adjusted man: no hard feelings, take care. So much so, I wonder if I made a mistake. After all, it's how a person reacts when the chips are down that matters. And Scrappy13's easy-going response makes him even more attractive.

Online dating can be a small, disappointing world.

I'm sure this is it. Dr.Dreamy is The One. So sure am I that I start to wonder what will become of my dating experiment. Will I be able to go on with it after being swept away in the wave of this man's perfect hair?

A block from Meze, where we're meeting, I see him. Forget that he took it upon himself to disprove my height-calculating formula by rounding up not two, but three inches; I can tell by his uncertain stance that he's actually not The One. He was so good on paper, but that's the unfortunate circumstance of dating online; you aren't privy to the nuances that make a person who he is: the confidence—or lack thereof, the chemistry—or lack thereof, the hair—or lack thereof. There was no full head of thick, spongy waves. Nope. He had a monk spot—a white beacon of bald capping off his dark curls.

It was apparent from a block away, but not at all in his pictures. I felt cheated by false advertising. It wasn't the crop circle on his head that did me in, though. Dr.Dreamy was meek. His handshake was limp, he wasn't sure about anything, including where to sit and what to drink, and I was forced to take the reins and propel our date into motion. Across the board, confidence might be the most important trait a guy can have. Dr.Dreamy left his at home, if he ever had it to begin with.

We're sitting on the patio at the edge of the sidewalk with the same vagina-armpit waiter as last week, and I almost tell Dr.Dreamy the CarrotTop story to liven up the utter boredom that is our conversation. I look up the street searching for something—anything—to talk about. And there's Scrappy13 walking toward us. With a woman. Shit. Shit. Shit. Shit. He sees me. Shit. What is he doing in my neighborhood? He's laughing, and I'm dying. There's not much to do in painful moments like this other than to ride them out. So, when Scrappy13 stops to say hi and shakes my hand with the same hand he used to feel me up in his car four days before, I pretend that this is the most normal coincidence ever. He introduces me to his friend Betsy, a redhead in a polka-dot shirt, and I introduce Betsy and Scrappy13 to Dr.Dreamy. There are more funny looks, nervous laughter, and general confusion from Betsy and Dr.Dreamy, who don't get the impossible awkwardness that is this moment. Did Scrappy13 think I broke it off with him to go out with Dr.Dreamy? Is he having the last laugh because he has full view of the blinding bald spot?

Like his last email to me though, Scrappy13 is laid back and unfazed. The unwelcome encounter becomes funny and not terrible at all. I almost want Scrappy13 and Betsy to join us, because at least I wouldn't be so bored. But they leave. I feel awful that I'm even on this date, not because I can already tell that I don't like Dr.Dreamy, but also because I'm uncomfortable going from one man to the next with hardly a breath in between. I'm also wondering if I made a mistake with Scrappy13. All I can think about is how, this time (in comparison to Dr. Dreamy), he looks really attractive.

The day after my date with Dr.Dreamy, which I allowed to turn into another three-hour marathon because he was so good on paper and I thought I should keep trying, TheKid called me on my commute home. My last online hope. He'd had knee surgery that morning and was on Vicodin—drug dialing. He was cute and charming with slurring giggles, but only at first.

"So my dad left to go pick up my prescription for stool softeners." He laughs. Then pauses. "Maybe I shouldn't have said that."

No, but I'm accommodating. "That's great your dad could come into town to help you out."

"Yeah. We've been hanging out. I can't really do anything so I've been sewing. I love to sew. Does that make me gay?" He squeaks. He's totally bombed.

"Yes, of course it does," I joke.

"No, no, no. I loooove women. I love everything about them." His voice quiets and he becomes sheepish. "And I love to nurse."

Silence. Lots and lots of silence.

I have no idea what to do with this one. I don't need clarification. The meaning is clear—he likes breasts and he likes to suckle them, like he did when I was learning long division. Maybe he's not talking actual lactating boobs; maybe he means foreplay nibbling and other acceptable second-base activities. I don't think he's suggesting role-playing in a tragic Oedipal way, or a scenario involving him wearing a diaper while engaging in said nursing. Or is he?

I realize it doesn't matter what shade of freak his fantasy falls under because I would never, ever be able to erase the image of him gurgling and cooing at my bosom. I don't begrudge TheKid his nursing, and I'm feeling prudish about my reaction, but it's a weird thing to drop on someone you haven't even kissed. Guys always seem to jump the gun, whether they're revealing their sexual preferences to you out of context like TheKid, grabbing boobs in cars as Scrappy13 did, blathering on about vaginal scents or forgetting that, in order to score a run, you have to spend time on every base. Why isn't someone covering this in tenth-grade health class?

TheKid emails me a few days later to ask if he went too far. I'd polled numerous friends and colleagues on this matter and received varied responses. Donna and Mike thought it was hilarious and couldn't stop laughing. Edie was confused and wanted to know exactly what he meant by nursing. Jeannine and Gabe thought I was making way too big a deal out of it. There was no consensus. I had to go with my gut. I send the breakup email.

And just like that, I'm single again.

Since I'd dated online prior to this experiment, it was a safe place to start, though I was much more aggressive this time around. If I had it all to do over, I would have been even more so. I would have spent less time applying my old dating method of hammering a square peg in a round hole with Scrappy13 and TheKid so I would have had more time to try out different men. Online dating is all about exploring the options.

Sometimes, though, it felt like I was picking through grounded apples rather than from the top of the tree. Still, I maintain that the Internet is a great way to meet people. I got my feet wet, didn't get too involved with anyone, and had the opportunity to be more proactive about dating. I'm not used to this level of activity, though. Making time for it was challenging and I had to set limits at the expense of other parts of my life to fit it in.

Expectations were the major stumbling blocks with online dating, and I needed to learn to keep mine in check. It was frustrating to get to know someone over email and then find out he didn't live up to the fantasy I'd created in my head about who he really was and what our relationship would be. Even pictures— the only concrete examples of who this person really is—are tough to decipher and not always reliable. Just like you have to account for height "fluctuations," a good rule of thumb for understanding what someone will look like is to take the worst picture from their profile and downgrade it two notches. Things can only get better from there. Or better yet, just use the profiles as a loose guide, and don't be so tied up in what someone looks like. (Right.)

It's time to switch things up. Next stop: singles events. Presumably, there's a better chance of finding someone with shared interests that actually might provide a foundation for a relationship. For example, events that entail dancing might produce single men who like to dance. I like to dance. I would like to meet someone who likes to dance. Dancing does not a relationship make, but it's a start.

There's no real reason for making this the next part of my experiment, except for (a) unlike online dating, I've never been to a singles event before, and (b) frankly, I'd like to get it over with. What kind of people go to these things, anyway?

Singles Events
A Lesson in Learning Not to Judge

'm doing another awkward postdate shuffle, this time at the base
of my front stoop. I make a circle on the concrete with the toe of
my silver flip-flop. Anything to avoid eye contact with The Bolivian. I met him earlier that night at a puu-puu platter singles event
put on by Pros in the City, one of the "largest social and networking
groups in the country," so says their website. The organization isn't
specifically a singles organization, but they do offer singles events
every week in their regular roster of daylong tubing trips, happy
hours, and summer jaunts to the Greek Islands. Our group of fifty
or so was split up into six smaller groups—three men and three
women—that took turns speed dating, gallery touring, and salsa
dancing with each other. And then The Bolivian and I went out
on our own date right after. And now my date is about to kiss me.

Some people say they love the anticipation and excitement of
a first kiss. Not me. I feel antsy and nervous, and my stomach

churns. This probably goes back to my first kiss, in freshman year of high school, which involved lots and lots of cold, slithery tongue, and I spit on the pavement afterward trying to excise the film of foreign saliva that had formed over my palate.[4] The kicker is that he broke up with me the next day and told everyone *I* was the bad kisser. Since then, I've worried about the first kiss with any guy because I'm anticipating the worst.

I continue to make circles on the concrete until The Bolivian leans in. And the kiss. Actually, it's more of a slurp on my top lip. It's not a bad technique per se, just different. I wonder if this is a Bolivian thing.

With his mouth on mine, I open my right eye to scan the street and sidewalk to make sure no one's around to witness our public display. But we're alone with the hissing air conditioners dangling from windows over the street.

I hadn't anticipated ending the singles event in an actual date. In fact, I'd assigned a fate of gloom and doom to the whole affair because, in addition to being scared off by large crowds of strangers, I was flying without a wingman. And the idea of being involved in a group that's engaged in orchestrated activities like speed dating? Not into that either. By nature, I'm not a joiner. I blame it on the fact that I never played team sports as a kid.

---

[4] Philematologists, who are scientists who study kissing, hypothesize that kissing probably developed as a way to transfer information to help us choose a mate with optimal genes that, when mixed with our own, create strong offspring. We're, in a sense, taste testing each other in an evolutionary effort to perpetuate our species.

I'd called the two single people I know and offered to foot the forty-dollar bill for their companionship and support. My rejection came in silences and chuckles. I was on my own, so I put on my game face (sheer lip gloss, pink blush with micro-sparkles, very black mascara) and black Target dress borrowed from Jeannine, chugged a beer, kissed my cat good-bye, and headed out to meet my fate with orange fur stuck to my lips.

Speed dating as Whack-a-Mole.

"Ever been to one of these things before?" Chuck, my first-ever speed date, blots the beaded sweat on his forehead with his cocktail napkin. His dark hair is folded into a layer of gel that's starting to unhinge in the foggy humidity. I peek around his shades, which look like they were plucked off a carousel at a West Virginia truck stop. Nope. Not cute. I'd been foiled again by the sunglasses.

I *chose* Chuck, though I would've eventually met him since the idea behind speed dating—the brainchild of a rabbi looking to hook up single Jews—is to rush through eight dates in one hour versus lingering on one date in three. When my group of women arrived on the roof deck of the Dupont Circle Hilton for this portion of the night, the men were already seated, three to a table. A voice from nowhere told us to pick someone to sit across from. As the other women coyly hung back, I took the lead and marched through the anticipating crowd. I'd uncovered a smidgen of confidence by making it to the meeting spot and not succumbing to the anxiety that was hovering right below my heart, ready to pounce, and I'd decided that if I was going to be here, I was going to make the best of it, dammit. Of course, I bypassed the guy I found most attractive because I didn't want to be too obvious, and sat down next to this less-intimidating would-be suitor.

"Nope. First time. You?" I'd witnessed speed dating at a restaurant where I was on a blind date a few years back and vowed never to do it. Too much nervous laughter and the bell ringing every four minutes to signal time to switch partners jangled my senses.

"Nope."

Behind the shades, his eyes shift to my chest, double-checking my nametag. But Chuck says nothing more.

I beat down the silence that settles on our conversation. Time's wasting. I think we get eight minutes per date, which is an eternity compared to the typical three- and four-minute speed dating events I'd seen advertised. I break my cardinal rule. "So. Chuck. What do you do?"

"I'm a systems analyst for the government."

It's about the most generic sounding job ever, and nothing he'll want to talk about or I'll understand. I'm prepared for this though because I'd seen the group of men from afar on the way to meet up with the female component of the event. Right then, I'd lowered my expectations to accommodate the Monet of khakis and pastel polos a block away. *Everyone* was probably a systems analyst here. I suppose it shouldn't matter what anyone does for a living. And I'm keeping an open mind, which was number one on the speed-dating hints I found online.

"What about you?"

"Oh, I work at a magazine, writing and editing." I switch my hand around in the air flippantly.

"Which one?"

"*Log Home Living*?" I say it like a question, squinting, even though I know he's never heard of it.

"What?"

"*Log Home Living*."

He looks confused, almost annoyed, like I might be toying with him. In the five years I've worked at the magazine, I've had this exact same conversation 312,467 times. "*Logs?*"

Sweet love.

"You know, like log homes? Abe Lincoln?" The Lincoln reference always clears everything up.

A wave of relief floods Chuck's face. He gets it. I'm not toying with him. And now that he has something to work with, he wants to know all about my job. I used to take great pleasure in discussing the nuances of log homes with strangers because it's funny to watch their expressions as they extrapolate how I got into the industry. It always goes something like this:

"So do you *own* a log home?"

"No, I rent a studio in the city."

Confused grimace, and, "Well, do you *want* to live in a log home?"

I explain the boring truth of how I wanted to work for a magazine and started there as a temp. The End. Chuck looks disappointed that there isn't something more. Like maybe I'm a direct descendant of Paul Bunyan, and Bart the Cat is actually a blue ox.

Before we have a chance to talk systems analysis, the Voice from Nowhere yells, "Switch!" Has it really been eight minutes?

Following Chuck, a stream of men filter in and out on cue, all stopping in at table fourteen to sit across from me for their prescribed time. With each "Switch!" the dates get shorter and shorter, and the whole damn exchange begins to feel like a game of Whack-a-Mole. Man pops up in the chair across from me; I whack him down with my mallet. Another pops up, *whack*. They keep coming faster and faster. Literally. There's no thinking. I concentrate on whacking anything that pops up in my field of vision. *Whack, whack, whack.*

By the time I make it to my final date, we've gone from eight- to two-minute dating. I read a statistic somewhere that it takes fifteen minutes for a man to decide if he wants to see a woman again. For women: one hour. However, I don't feel like I'm missing out on another fifty-two minutes to see if I *really* like a single one of these men, because like my online dates, it feels like I'm picking through a bushel of bruised apples of all shapes, sizes, and ages.

Back with the girls in the elevator, the mood hovers barely above a whimper. A redhead in skinny jeans and pointy heels sums up all of our thoughts. "Slim pickings." Heads bob slowly and quietly with more than a hint of disappointment.

On the walk over to the gallery for the second part of the event with a new crop of men to weed-wack through, I play with the idea of ditching. The event isn't the least bit structured and I wouldn't be missed. Keep an open mind, I remind myself. This is an *experiment*. I'm just trying it out. Investigating. And besides, I really like the women I'm meeting.

The new group of men my group of ladies will mingle with are already in full swing at the gallery, plastic cups filled to the one-inch ration mark with chardonnay. They'd come from salsa lessons.

I march directly over to the makeshift bar, urge the volunteer to fill my cup to the brim, and merge into the group of perspiring hairlines and armpits, sipping and spilling wine down the front of my dress. The scene here is less Whack-a-Mole and more *Where the Wild Things Are*. At speed dating, guys were told what table to go to and when to move and women just had to sit and wait. Now it's a free-for-all and the testosterone is revved up a few notches from the Latin dancing. Some men are eyeing the prospects while the brave ones have left the pride and have eased into conversations with the gazelles prancing into the museum.

I watch the guy with basketball player shoulders intercept Perfect Redhead. I hang back while they introduce themselves to gauge whether or not I stand a chance with him. Of course I don't. They're the alpha couple—the beautiful ones. I hunt for other options and zero in on Slim, who appears to be the runt of the litter. Short, bony, hunched over, gaze rooted six feet down. He is absolutely the least threatening person in the room.

Going out with him would be what my friend Patrick calls "dating down." Patrick is my L.A. friend. Patrick does not date down. Patrick dates beautiful size-four (or smaller) women who are exactly in his aesthetic league.

It is Slim's lack of presence, or perhaps his vulnerability and my biological calling to lick wounds, that makes him the most approachable. That and I have nothing to lose because I am absolutely not interested. I walk over to him, stick out my hand to shake his, and introduce myself.

Slim looks up and smiles meekly.

He's exactly how I thought he'd be: pleasant, but without a shred of confidence. I regret my choice to talk to him immediately, and within ninety-six seconds I've targeted a square-jawed possibility across the room. I need to wiggle myself out of this foxhole that I've jumped into. I could implement my trusty Plan Pee, where I excuse myself to the ladies' room while he inevitably finds someone else to talk to. But I don't want to do that. I want to talk to someone—anyone—else. And there's nothing wrong with that. That's why we're all here.

I pack up my guilt and prepare to move on. "Well, it was nice to meet you. Think I'm gonna walk around and check out the rest of the exhibit." I smile as I place my hand on his arm, just above the elbow, and tilt my head as sort of an apology for abandoning him.

Five steps to the left and Carlos, a tall Argentinean in trainers and plaid pants, swoops in.

"Hi, how are you?" His voice whispers like there's a wad of phlegm caught in the back of his throat. There's an easy way about him. He tells me I have an easy way about me.

"Well, that's 'cause I'm bombed." I bat my eyelashes shamelessly. The thin layer of ice between us melts. I can't tell if I'm attracted to this man, but I like his style and there's something about him that screams *good in bed*.

"Give me your palm." Carlos says he has been studying palmistry and he gently takes hold of my hand, turning it around in his dry, cracked fingers that look as if they work with heavy tools all day. More people filter into our conversation, but not in an attempt to break up our momentum. We're just talking. There are no attention grabbers, no agenda followers, and no wildebeests goring any trees—just a few singletons enjoying the evening. Dare I say that I'm having a delightful time? Is it possible that I could be a singles-event person?

At the final happy-hour mixer, after the salsa lessons where I danced with seven different guys, all with the grace of a blind, three-legged bulldog, I nab two prospects. One is The Pilot, who looks frighteningly like my ex (The Ex) and gives me his phone number, though we won't get together for a couple of weeks because of his flight schedule. Two is The Bolivian, who took me straight out to Tabaq on U Street, where it's wall-to-wall World Bank twentysomethings who think they're in Ibiza. Men in tight shirts and clunky watches leer at women with panels of stick-straight hair and gold hoop earrings. The Bolivian and I are off in the corner of the roof deck. The view is the Washington Monument and a sliver moon. It's phallic and mildly romantic.

He orders a bottle of Cristal, flips his head back, and wipes his black curls out of his eyes. "You're lucky you're out with me on T.B. Day."

The blood in my veins had come to a standstill when I calculated what I'd owe if I'm paying for half of a bottle of Cristal. But now I'm confused. T.B. Day?

T.B. are his initials. "Me day. Once a month I treat myself to a special day where I do nice things for myself like drink champagne."

"And go to lame singles events?"

"Well, I met you, didn't I?" He's almost charming. Up until now, I wasn't quite sure what I was doing with him. I wasn't interested in him at the mixer. He just happened to act fast and sweep me up in the idea of dinner before I had a chance to realize I might want to say no. And I was hungry. And I was into the fact that he was trying so hard with me.

Champagne is flowing like a P. Diddy happy hour and I'm drinking liberally even though I can't quite get the fork to my lips and have spilled what seems to be guacamole all over Jeannine's dress. But it's so dark, who can tell? How did I get so drunk? I attempt to tally up all the drinks I've consumed. Nope. Can't. Too drunk.

"Should we go dancing?" The Bolivian's eyes are sparkling and his nervous energy seems to have subsided. "I saw you out there at the salsa lessons. For a gringa, you can move." His knee brushes mine under the table and my spine prickles.

I blush. "How come you weren't dancing?" I saw him at the lessons, too. He'd looked down his nose at everyone from his perch at the bar.

"I don't need salsa lessons." Not an ounce of humor in his tone. It's a straight shot of Latino machismo.

He's kind of a prick, but the champagne is good and he seems to like me. There's something about him.

So I let The Bolivian whip me around the dance floor at Habana Village, a salsa club in my neighborhood that I've always wanted to go to but never have because I don't want to go alone. And then he slurped my lip on my front stoop while I gloated with a sense of satisfaction about the whole night. I'd conquered a gripping fear by going out on my own, drank ridiculously expensive champagne, and got to go dancing. It wasn't nearly as bad as my nerves had anticipated. Not bad at all.

In the midst of my self-congratulation, The Bolivian slides his hand across my breast. What is it with the boob grabbing? It's bad manners and it's not meant for my pleasure. I think it's meant to let me know that if I wasn't about to invite him upstairs, I might as well now, because, hey, we already made it to second base. Or, maybe it's a longer-term strategy so that if we do see each other again, he can go straight to feeling me up and not waste any time with the warm-up. Or maybe it's not premeditated. This sounds more accurate since there doesn't appear to be any thought to the maneuver—he's just grabbing willy-nilly. See boob. Must grab. Now.

I pull away, smile, and say good night. He promises to call. I don't care. He must have tuned into my ambivalence. Men have such a funny way of knowing when women couldn't care less. And their knee-jerk reaction is to keep close contact. The thrill of the chase. He texts me when he gets home. And the next morning. Then he emails. Then he calls. I can't help but love the attention, but . . . There's that *but*.

This *but* was all I needed to determine one date was enough with The Bolivian. But, then I started to overanalyze. I kept thinking that maybe I was missing something, that maybe he deserved another chance. Maybe our first date wasn't enough to know.

Our second date—a feeble attempt to re-create the first right down to the bottle of Cristal and salsa dancing—didn't go so well. I thought when he showed up in a Cadillac with a driver that this indicated that there was some sort of adult foundation to work with. But he was thirty going on thirteen, and he threw out red flags all over the playing field while I gingerly tiptoed around them: revoked license from a couple DUIs (hence car with driver), an ex-girlfriend from high school who still haunts him, didn't have a plan for our date, snapped at the waitstaff. These were crucial peepholes into his person, and they were turnoffs. Even the wee drink-umbrella-sized red flags (empty cans of Red Bull littering the floor of the Caddy, playing "Rock You Like a Hurricane" on the way over to the restaurant) should have had me sprinting in the other direction.

Unfortunately, all of it also sounded off the wounded-dog alarm that's music to my caretaking ears, and I couldn't turn away. We'd already established a relationship pattern: he'd get irritated, I'd assuage his colic, and we'd both drink as much as we could as quickly as possible. So I brought my vulnerable, lost, and confused stray home with me.

When I let The Bolivian stay over, I'd laid the ground rules: Just cuddling. But then, I found lots of reasons why it was okay to shelve my no-sex-on-the-second-date rule, though the precoital third-person references to his superman stamina and come-ons like "You know you want to" should have stopped me cold in my tracks. But our compatibility horoscope said the sex could be good, and I'd decided that this—us—was going nowhere, so I didn't have to worry about wanting him to like me later on. Oh, the justifications one can rip out of thin air for having loveless premarital sex.

I drive The Bolivian home the next morning (after taking him to Burger King at his request), thinking if I treated this like a girlfriend dropping off her boyfriend, I wouldn't feel so tawdry. Especially knowing I have another date in about four hours.

Frisbee Guy had emailed me through the Onion, where I'd kept up my profile in case someone amazing came along. I couldn't say no. He was cute, my age, just moved back to the states from Russia. And he was up for playing Frisbee.

I meet Frisbee Guy at Malcolm X Park, right before a rainstorm. He's sitting on the steps that lead up to the grassy field and I toss the Frisbee to him as soon as he looks up from under his baseball cap. It's a miserable throw from only ten feet away and he has to chase it down.

We're laughing. This is a fun start. His face is rounder and his hair is thinner than in his pictures but he has beautiful green eyes. As soon as we shake hands, the sky opens. We find cover under an old elm and talk until the rain clears. I'm almost sad it does, because sitting and talking under a tree in the middle of a rainstorm is so romantic. Frisbee Guy is so easygoing. I could have hung out there with him all afternoon. But Frisbee is the agenda and it was my idea. I can't back out now.

"I have to warn you, I'm really not that good." I love to play Frisbee and talk about playing Frisbee, but I can't really back up my enthusiasm for it with any sort of skill. And the neighborhood kids who ask if they can play with us are worse. They take over the game with wobbly, off-course throws that barely miss slamming into homeless people sleeping on benches. It's all a little awkward, because obviously you can't talk while playing Frisbee, and even if we could, we wouldn't be able to because we're too busy babysitting.

It gets better later, when Frisbee Guy and I drink Chimay at L'Enfant and swap online dating stories. It's one of those afternoons that could easily melt right into the night. But we both have plans. It's probably better anyway, I think. Quit while we're ahead. This is the best date I've had since starting this experiment and I don't want to ruin it. We double-cheek kiss good-bye and I practically skip home with a free spirit from feeling like someone actually gets me.

Sometimes you have to set the lowest bar first.

More than two years ago, I signed up to get emails from a group called Single Volunteers of D.C. (SVDC), but still hadn't made it to one of their events. Blame it on a busy schedule. Blame it on the notices in bolded red font for most event listings that always seem to say *Full for women! Need more men!!!!* Blame it on a group shot from a zoo cleanup day on their website. Dumpy, dowdy, skinny, bad hair, too old. My list for opting out is shallow and long. But I always say I want to volunteer, that I want to give back. So, I throw in my superficial towel.

And I pick it right back up when I get to the meeting place near Freedom Plaza early on Sunday morning to volunteer for a lupus walk. Hair-sprayed Holly Hobby helmets, acid wash, and bright white sneakers blind my bleary eyes. I want to pile this motley crew into my Hyundai for a trip to the mall for makeovers and a shopping spree. *This* could be my contribution.

I meet three men right away. There's Joe, a spacey fiftysomething who disappears around the corner not to be seen or heard from for most of the event; Frank, the guy who goes to all of the events and is chatty and loud and makes a point of knowing everyone; and Toby, who stands next to me in our circle of fifteen single helpers. He's a blond-haired, blue-eyed transplant from Arizona who takes the purple volunteer bandana we're all supposed to wear and ties it around his head.

"Gangstah style." He says this oblivious to the crowd of African American walkers who might actually take offense to his ridiculous attempt at street slang, though really, they'd probably laugh and shake their heads at the poor white boy. He's goofy, yes, but relative to the other men here, he seems to be the best option.

I stand by Toby and Frank. I don't think I could ever be interested in either of them, but they seem to be the most normal of all the men and I don't want to go near the women. I've concluded that they all hate me because no one has invited me into their conversation.

After roll call, we stand and wait because there's nothing for us to do yet. Neither of the reasons for me being here (finding a date and volunteering) is coming into fruition. I'm impatient as the group ambles over to a Starbucks for coffee, where I latch on to Kathy, a suburban gal who lacks pretense. She doesn't hate me like the other girls, and jokes about how these events never seem to have viable men. "But it's good to be around other single people."

I guess. Being on the mission that I am, though, I don't feel quite as forgiving.

When Kathy runs to the bathroom, I'm left to wander alone because there's still nothing to do. So I lean against a table within proximity of the group to sip on my decaf and eat a croissant. By the last drop of coffee, I'm still standing alone. I'm frozen like a deer in headlights, scared to move lest it's a leap right into danger. What if I walk up to someone and he (or she) ignores me? The worst that could happen: I get laughed off Freedom Plaza. And if I did, I'd be really embarrassed until I got to the bus stop. Then I would go home and call every last person in my cell phone contact list to tell them how I got laughed off of Freedom Plaza and that it was the *last* time I'd *ever* think about volunteering again.

The group has broken off into mini conversations. Frank continues to talk and talk and talk while Toby nods his head and rearranges his purple headband. Acid-wash Darren has center stage with two women, three other gals from the group are gabbing like old friends, and Holly Hobby is sitting alone dejectedly on the curb. She reminds me of Slim, and normally I'd head straight for her since she's the least threatening. But her energy is toe up. I steer clear and merge awkwardly into Frank and Toby's tête-à-tête.

"So, you come to these events a lot?" I direct this at Frank because he's the one I'm least interested in and seems easiest to talk to.

"Yeah, they're fun. And it's nice to hang out with other single people." His lispy squawk is honest and unapologetic. Maybe I have it all wrong. Singles events *aren't* just about dating, but about meeting and hanging out with like-minded people, like a new-moms group or log-home lovers. And these people can give me one thing that not many people can: the feeling that I'm not the only single one out there, which can be stifling and lonely no matter how nice it is to get to sleep in the middle of the bed and not check in with anyone every time I want to go for a run. At singles events, I'm not the third or fifth or seventh wheel.

There's a post-volunteering brunch where more connections can be made. But I can't go. I've double booked myself with a bartending class where I *know* there will be cute guys. I just know it.

Wrong.

I think I'm so smart. Yet sitting on an ancient swivel stool with leather splinters cutting into my thigh, a lone isle off the coast of an archipelago of twosomes, threesomes, and foursomes, I realize I know nothing. I paid forty dollars to drive to Nowheresville, Maryland, for this bartending class slash singles event, only to be surrounded by gaggles of girly girls, a frat-boy duo, the Jimmy Buffett trio (not a band—they just looked like the type of people who would love Jimmy Buffett: late thirties, beer paunches, Hawaiian shirts), and two couples decked out in khakis and white linen. I wonder if they planned their outfits so no one would break up their L.L.Bean bliss.

Across the room, I spy a few potential errant wheels like me, but the solidarity I had started to feel with my fellow volunteers at the lupus walk is gone. I miss Frank, Toby, and Holly, and wish they were here for more commiserating. Didn't the thingstodo .com website label the class as a singles event? I thought for sure it did. And I thought for sure it would attract single singles like me, not groups of singles and definitely not groups of couples. And there are no men I'm attracted to except for the one that's married, of course. Do single men in D.C. not care about how to mix a proper Cosmo? Of course they don't. They pop beers or sip bourbon and water. Why would they need to know how to mix a drink unless they had a wife with friends for whom they would bartend on a girls' night?

At the end of a long day of meeting no one special, I started to compile a mental list of things I'd rather do than go to a singles event. Sitting on my toilet seat and picking dead skin off my toes came to mind. Cleaning out the litter box was another. And if faced with the would-you-rather dilemma of singles event versus a dinner party with my former online loves, I would have immediately called for a reservation for five, though it seems terribly unfair that I'd have to choose between such unpalatable options.

This is when I started to lower my expectations, because if this was all I was going to get to choose from, I felt like I needed to choose *something*.

Weak vibes are signals, too.

The Pilot talks into his menu. "I wonder what ceviche is."

"Fish. Marinated in lemon or lime juice." Doesn't everyone know what ceviche is?

I'd already been trying not to judge him for not having a plan for our date, even though he had two whole weeks to pull something together since we'd met at the Pros in the City event. People have planned weddings in less time. It's been my experience that a man's interest is not only determined by whether or not he pays, but is also directly correlated to how he plans his dates. One time, I went out with a guy who made three reservations ahead of time and when he came to pick me up, he simply asked, "Italian, French, or Chinese?" I picked Italian, and he called to cancel the other two. He wanted to impress me. I liked that.

With The Pilot, we made a loose plan to meet up on the sidewalk in my neighborhood, and when we did, he shrugged his shoulders over where we should go, hiding behind the fact that he just moved here. I decided that reminding him about the existence of the Internet and all the nifty ways you can search for restaurants and things to do wasn't very nice. So I picked the restaurant.

Despite my misgivings, I cut The Pilot a break since I've had a hard time coming to terms with the physical appearance of the men I've dated, and he looks pretty darn appealing. So much so that I almost don't care that he's definitely shorter than me and wears jeans that taper at the ankle. Seated at a nice patio table, we pull our budding relationship out of the dormancy it had fallen into, and the server has to come back three times before we're ready to order because we're just talking and talking and talking.

"I think we're ready now. But first, what's your name?" The Pilot sticks out his right hand to our server.

"Jose."

"Hey, Jose! Great to meet you!" He shakes his hand and then introduces me to Jose like they've been besties for years. Okaaaaay. I like that he's social, and being friendly to waitstaff is crucial. But this is overkill. Social quirks aside, The Pilot is polite, well-mannered, and a good conversationalist. And impressively, he owns five houses in various states, which seems like overkill but is also kind of appealing.

After our plates are cleared, Jose lays the check directly between us. He couldn't have centered it more accurately if he'd had a ruler. The Pilot and I glance at the pleather billfold like it's the elephant in the room it's about to become. There are so many schools of thoughts on this: man always pays, whoever asks pays, go Dutch, woman offer/man reject. And then you have to take into account what it all means. A man who pays definitely likes you. A man who forces bill-splitting doesn't. A woman who insists on paying probably doesn't like the man she's with and doesn't want to feel like she owes him anything. And a woman who lets a man pay without so much as a look toward her purse is a gold digger. I usually err on the side of woman offer/man reject, even though it's a silly exercise and I think that on the first date the man should pay. Up until now, they have. So I wait. He opens the bill. "Let's pay and get outta here."

Let's. He said, "Let's." I guess since he never technically asked me to dinner—it was a plan to "get together" that barely evolved—we should go Dutch. I don't really believe this, but I go for the pseudo purse grab in case "let's" really means "let us" and not "let me."

I remember the singles event when, instead of buying me a drink, The Pilot handed over a ten-dollar bill and said, "For mine." At that point, the back of my brain was hissing "lame" to the front of my brain singing "let's see how it goes." I know now how this is going to go. But I didn't think it would be as annoying as it turned out.

"You had the polenta and I had the flank steak . . ." He's itemizing! My heart drops into my stomach. I root around in my purse, stalling and giving him the chance to make it right.

". . . we shared the ceviche, so we can split that . . ."

"It's cool. Just split it down the middle." I smile convincingly, pull out my debit card that will be depleted of the $59.82 I have to my name for the next ten days, and toss it over to the billfold because I can't seem to reach all the way across the table. It's as if my arms have shrunk into the vestigial limbs of a T. rex because I really truly believe he should pick up the tab.

The Pilot glances up from the wad of twenties and fifties he's unfurling between his fingers. "Are you sure?" He looks worried. But what am I going to say? No, Mr. Pilot Land Baron, *you* pay.

I nod and smile some more. "Yeah. No worries."

"Well, do you want me to give you cash and you can put it all on your card?"

There's something utterly vulgar about this idea. I shake my head vigorously over The Pilot's unwitting call to put me in the red. I couldn't feel less special at this point, but I still attempt an open mind through after-dinner drinks and the walk home.

"I like you. I'd really like to see you again." He's so earnest standing there, smiling at me. This is what I like about him. He's straightforward and honest. I stop ruminating over why he didn't offer to pay and why, over our nightcap beers, he started to talk about penis rings.

We hug. He tucks his elbows into his sides instead of around my back and there's a two-foot space buffer between our bodies. He's smiling sweetly at me—too sweetly. Any inkling of kissing him has completely gone out the window. I might as well be saying good night to someone's grandmother who has sent me home with a batch of warm cookies.

I barge into Kenneth's apartment to recap. I sink into his couch next to him, perplexed. "Do you think he's gay?" I ask after I dump all the details on him. I'm jumping the gun, but I did get a gay vibe after the weak hug.

Kenneth is crashed out, an empty bottle of merlot in front of him on the coffee table. He's not interested in debating sexuality. "Hooker, he's *cheap*. Do *not* go out with him again. You're too good for that."

"I know." I don't actually think I know, but I'm exhausted. Defeated.

"If you really liked him, his not paying wouldn't be that big of a deal," Jeannine, the voice of reason, tells me on her couch over veggie tacos the next night. "Sometimes it's easier to pick on the superficial stuff."

There *are* other things that are problematic about The Pilot. The earnest, bright-eyed, and bushy-tailed thing is endearing, but I have a feeling it will get old. Fast. That seems so picky though. What's wrong with dating a really nice guy? He's a catch. I should like him.

My gut has one opinion on the matter (and it sounds a lot like Kenneth) and my head, another. Should I give it another chance? I'm torn. So I do nothing. I'll just wait and see. It might be impossible to gauge true compatibility with someone on the first date. But at the same time, when your gut is telling you to run, sometimes you just want to run. I have to consider, though, that maybe my gut is telling me to run because I'm afraid of getting involved with someone with whom I could actually forge a real relationship.

I do run—straight to The Bolivian's place on Sunday for a bizarre afternoon at his rooftop pool. We lounge side by side with not much to talk about, working backward trying to form something other than a physical connection while watching a real couple swim around, hugging and kissing. Only later, back at his apartment after Thai takeout, does he start his seduction scene, scooting closer to me on the couch and pulling my feet into his lap. He inspects my legs.

"You're pretty, but your legs aren't perfect." I look down at the leftover scars on my shins from eczema, and dusty feelings of embarrassment creep over me. I spent most of my life covering up to hide my skin, and absorbed consistent ridicule in childhood and even into adulthood. Now, The Bolivian is dredging up those feelings of insecurity and I think the reason he's doing it is because he's insecure, too. We are a bad, bad match.

The realization has finally dawned on me that this is going nowhere. I won't take him making me feel insecure. I will break it off with him as soon as I get up the nerve, which is after three weeks of telling him I'm too busy to see him.

I postpone all dates until the next weekend so I can pull myself together. Hibernating in the middle of the summer isn't my thing. But it's a needed respite from the coordinating, texting, calling, emailing, and bouncing around I've been doing. Dating has officially become my second job and I need some time off.

Second dates do not create chemistry.

The Pilot smiles widely and waves. "Hey!" He stands on the other side of the railing dividing the sidewalk and the restaurant patio where we're meeting for brunch; he's sweating through his orange T-shirt.

"Hi! Were you just running?"

"Yeah. Ten miles! I'm in training!" He looks around for the gate opening to let him on the patio.

"You gotta walk around." I point at the front door.

He looks at the door, sizes up the three-foot railing, and leaps. He almost makes it, but clips his toes and goes body first into the table next to me. Tables heave, white plastic chairs overturn, water glasses shatter, and parents with kids glare. It's mayhem. I bow my head and wrap my hands around the back of my neck while he rights himself. "Sorry about that." He apologizes to the family, who is abhorred by his gall, and carefully seats himself as the waitress with the skinny gray braids that have seen many stacks of flapjacks approaches our table to take our order. "Honey, what can I get for you?"

I deliberately order light and cheap. I'm not testing him, exactly. I'm simply creating an easy situation for him to take me out. Maybe all of his money is tied up in real estate. I don't mind eating light so our kids can have a future. "Two eggs, over hard, rye toast."

She jots and eyes The Pilot for his order.

"What's your name?" Lord almighty. He's introducing himself

again. And me. She plays along but I can just hear Miss Mary's inner monologue saying, "Now, he's a strange man."

The Pilot emerges from a trip to the bathroom bearing our plates from the kitchen. "Breakfast is served!" Miss Mary is right behind him with a bowl of cantaloupe, shaking her braids in a combination of amusement and annoyance. Sister, I feel the same way.

"Two eggs and toast for the lady." He presents my breakfast to me with a flourish.

He's so pleased with himself. It *is* charming. But still, I shift in my chair as if there were a nail sticking right into my sciatic nerve.

A German shepherd walking by, who might have been born the same year as Moses and who has lost control over his mucus membrane, sticks his gray nose through the rails under our table. His owner, equally ancient and wearing a matching red bandana, is right behind him.

"What's his name?" The Pilot reaches down to pet the dog that slobbers all over his hand.

Crickey. Even the dogs. He wants to meet *everyone*.

The Pilot offers his water glass to his new friend Bruno, who slurps and sprays all over our legs. When Bruno and his dad carry on, The Pilot sets the glass, now coated in milky canine juices, on the table.

"You'd better move that over here in case you forget." I gingerly pick up the glass and place it off to the side by the sugar and syrup.

"Oh, I won't forget."

Oh, he forgot.

Three minutes later, he reaches for the dog water. I look at him, eyebrows raised, mouth open, about to tell him to stop. But he's already chugging. Downing the murky dog water. He sees my reaction, looks cross-eyed into his glass, and stops drinking. He shrugs. "Dog's mouths are cleaner than humans anyway."

"Not *that* dog's mouth." I'm laughing.

He grabs the edge of the table and leans in. "On that note, ready?"

He picks up the bill that Miss Mary left for us and we take it to the register, where I pay ten dollars on my four-dollar meal because he suggested that with tip and tax, I would owe that much anyway. Why is it the person who always orders and owes the least ends up paying more? It's infuriating, though I don't know if my reaction is really about him not paying for me. Maybe it is an easy-out excuse so I don't have to dig around inside my feelings to understand why I'm so turned off.

Doesn't matter. I break it off with The Pilot a week after the dog-water date. I called him after a pep talk from Kenneth that went something like: "Honey, he's *cheap*. Call him and get it over with."

Kenneth was right. If there's anyone who understands his worth, it's Kenneth. He's great at demanding what he deserves. I suppose I think I deserve whatever and whoever comes along, even if it's not wholly satisfying. No more. I will not settle for cute but cheap (with tapered jeans). I call The Pilot while standing on the front stoop because I have no cell reception in my apartment.

"So listen. I probably should've said this before, but I kinda feel like this is more friends than anything else." I'm pacing the three-foot stoop and making cryptic gestures with my free hand. We'd been making idle chitchat and I finally had an opening to get on with my "I'm not feeling it" speech.

"Oh. So what you're saying is that you're not interested in dating me."

Yes. That's exactly what I'm saying. Did he really need to recap?

"Yeah. I'm sorry. I don't want to lead you on." My face is squished waiting for the blow.

"Well, I appreciate your being honest. I actually don't feel like this is just friends. But that's okay. Call me if you change your mind!"

That was it. This might be the easiest breakup ever.

Despite the fact that he's jobless, Frisbee Guy pays. And then *I* pay the next time. And then he pays. We have a nice momentum and go on a few more dates, which all revolve around a lot of drinking (sake and sushi, beer and baseball, afternoon PBRs at the coffeehouse) and a lot of talking about sex. Not sex between us, but how Americans are prudish about sex and Europeans aren't. He has the ex-pat chip on his shoulder, which I totally understand. When I got back from traveling abroad, I carried it around for a few months, too. America is *so close-minded*. But really. Get over it.

Frisbee Guy doesn't require a breakup. I think he gets how noncommittal I feel about him since, as we progressed in number of dates, I would cut them off earlier and earlier and I'd only respond to his texts and emails in whimpers and half-starts. Eventually, I never hear from him again. Even though I knew exactly what happened, I still wondered what happened. Even though

I didn't like him enough, I still wanted him to like me. To want me. To pursue me.

By the end of the summer, I have one last hope. Rafe. Like Frisbee Guy, he's a straggler from the Onion, which I can't seem to pull my profile down from because I miss the day-to-day excitement of online browsing. His wink came mid-Bolivian and Pilot, but we already knew each other from an email liaison six months before. It lasted two weeks until I ceased talks before we ever met because I met someone I thought I liked better. This time Rafe has better pictures up and wants to start all over again. We chalk it up to bad timing and pick up where we left off.

But then his emails stop as we were making tentative plans to get together. Is this calculated retribution? Sort of. Rafe met someone else. He wants to see where it goes. He's sorry.

I never met Rafe, but I cried anyway. I cried for our relationship that never was but that, in my mind, would've been so perfect. I cried because I'm tired of running around dating and trying to make something work with someone (anyone). I cried for all the letdowns and disappointments over the past three months—for the men who couldn't live up to the ideal that I have so firmly etched on my brain. The ideal that no one could possibly live up to and that most likely keeps me from having to get involved with anyone. And I cried because it occurred to me that maybe I'm not capable of having a relationship because I wouldn't know a good man if he chased me down. (I kept forgetting that, actually, my goal isn't to meet The One. It's to test out dating. Meeting The One would muck it all up.) And really, why can't I simply have fun dating? Just because it doesn't turn into a long-term relationship doesn't mean it's a failure.

My family's annual sojourn to sand and sloth on the Delaware shore came just in time. I needed a break from dating and thinking about men, trying to understand men and my feelings about men. But then, on my first day there, at the dunes, I randomly brushed by Dave Grohl of the Foo Fighters. I'd nearly convinced myself at one point that we would end up together in one of those weird celebrity fantasies you concoct in your head when there's no one in real life to think about. Dave Grohl was on vacation with his family, too, and they were staying in one of those enormous beach houses right on the water. My heart flipped when I recognized the tattooed arms and neck and realized it was him. I seriously thought fate had made me single for that moment, the moment that would so inevitably lead to Dave Grohl singing "Everlong" to me until his tattoos were faded and sagging.

And then he turned to beckon to his wife, who was eight months pregnant. I was yanked out of my desperate fantasy world and thrust into the reality of a rusty lounge chair by the sea and three months of *New Yorker*s to catch up on, wishing I had one *US Weekly*.

I ended up going to two other singles events for this part of the experiment—speed dating for tall men and women who love them, and a scavenger hunt—and the results were the same goofy, awkward interaction as all the others before. And they culminated in exactly zero dates. The rejection email I received after the tall-men event was the worst. At the end, everyone checked off a form with whom they're interested in, and all the forms were matched up. This is what I got:

> Based on the mutual matching system you did not make any mutual matches. This is not to say that nobody checked you as a potential match, but you did not express interest in anyone that did so.

Basically, it was my fault for being too picky and only checking off two guys. And it was. It wasn't just unrealistic expectations keeping me down. I'm still wrestling with my wanting the men I date to look a certain way, and until I get past that, I'll have to get used to the feeling of not having many choices. On a positive note, I won a ten-dollar Target gift certificate when my team finished the scavenger hunt first. And I can now mix a mean Long Island Iced Tea. And I uncovered confidence I didn't know I had by simply showing up at these things on my own. Contrary to what I thought might happen, I did not curl up and die a painful, torturous death.

In addition to not dying, I appreciated being able to test chemistry right off the bat, unlike with online dating where predicting chemistry is next to impossible. Still, I didn't find much of a spark anyway because the pool of men I was fishing around in was limited both in numbers (ten to twenty-five men total with each event, some not even single), and I felt like I was seeing the same guys over and over again, just like I felt after a month of dating online, and I was doing more weeding and whacking than anything.

In theory, I like the idea of expanding my circle, of being around like (i.e., single) people. But the reality is, I already have a broad social network and it does include single people like me. As one friend said when I asked him if he'd ever go to a singles event: "Why would I pay to go to something like that when I can go to a bar and do the same thing with my friends?"

I'm glad to leave singles events behind and try something new—blind dates. I'd started to put out the word to friends and one thing is certain: My date and I will have at least one thing in common.

Blind Dates

A Lesson in Being Open to the Possibilities

I have twenty minutes to decide what I'm going to wear before I'm late to meet Lorenzo. At this point, you'd think I'd have a trusty date outfit established that I could pluck out of my closet at a moment's notice. Today, I'm working with an extra five pounds but feeling like it's twenty, and it will require me to try on every last piece of clothing I own and endure a lengthy mental flagellation for not eating less and exercising more. The selection of pants that offer enough room is narrowed down to one pair of jeans, and I try on all my summer tops with those jeans to feel like I have some choices. I pull a blouse from the heaping pile of cotton and silk on my bed. It's gauzy, it's white, it's ruffled; it will do.

I primp and preen, while trying not to look too primped and preened, and check every five-degree angle of my butt in the mirror. I don't know why I have to do this every time I leave my apartment, and sometimes I do it when I'm just hanging out at home. I'm in a constant state of neurotic wonder over the size of my ass, and rarely do I ever consider that if I used the time I spent inspecting myself doing squats or lunges instead, perhaps my ass wouldn't feel or look so enormous.

Four minutes to go. I check my lip gloss for errant cat hairs and head out down my usual path to the strip of bars and restaurants in my neighborhood that's slowly becoming less international and eclectic and more fraternity row. I pass the Christ House, a stop-over for sick and homeless people. I usually gauge how I look by the number of hellos I get from the old men hanging out on the patio smoking menthols and chatting each other up. I'm greeted by a bald guy with skin like a black olive. He's propped up in a wheelchair, one foot tucked in a bright white sock, the other foot missing, cigarette dangling from cracked lips, and a boom box to his ear. "Mmm. Hell-oh there." He says it over the purr of Al Green, smiling at me through a stream of smoke.

When I look down shyly, I see light purple lace patterns bob-bing around underneath my filmy top. I forgot to switch to my nude-colored bra. Crap.

I can't go home to change. I'm already going to be five minutes late. I trudge on and decide to pretend that I *meant* to have my pretty bra showing through.

The restaurant, which looks like the set of *The Jetsons,* is empty except for one guy seated at the bar.

"Hey!" Lorenzo stays seated and we shake hands. He's much better looking than his picture, which I had him send even though this flies in the face of blind dating. His hair, complexion, and eyes are warm shades of brown, and he's wearing a button-down and khaki shorts that seem to swallow him whole. He's definitely not taller than me, but I knew this would be the case because I had deduced it from one of the pictures he sent.

Lorenzo's handshake is solid, but he doesn't seem as confident as he was over email. He seems nervous. Maybe it's first-date jitters. Maybe he doesn't like purple lace bras.

Halfway through our first beer, I've covered his vital stats: pulse—check; fully clothed—check; grew up in Northern Virginia—check; divorced parents—check; siblings—check.

Lorenzo deadpans, "Has Wendy ever touched you funny? You gotta watch her."

Wendy is my chiropractor who set us up. I'm not expecting this line of conversation, but I go with it. "Sometimes she rubs my butt, but I'm *sure* she's just doing her job."

He laughs, looking at me sideways. I sip beer. He sips beer. "I wouldn't be so sure of that."

He's funny, but as we talk, I take everything I learn about him and turn it into something I'm not interested in. Presumably, I'm putting up boundaries by assigning negative feelings to benign things like his preferences for jam bands and golf. I overlook the fact that Lorenzo has an easygoing vibe, that he befriended the bartender before I even got to the bar, but not in an annoying way like The Pilot, that he makes me laugh, and that he likes cats. He even offers to train Bart to stay off the kitchen counters, which I have failed at miserably time and again.

The real problem is that my heart isn't in it today. Sundays are for brunches with friends, reading the paper over lattes with an established boyfriend, or lying on the couch with Bart.

The check comes and Lorenzo pulls it to his side without blinking. I may have skimmed over his other positive traits, but *this* I notice. It's amazing how this casual move changes everything. And after The Pilot, it's refreshing.

Outside on the sidewalk, slouching into my shirt because of the bra issue and sinking into my shoes because of the height issue, I thank Lorenzo for dinner.

We hug. There's not *not* a spark. I don't *not* like him.

What's wrong with me? Why am I so picky?

I find an answer in an unlikely source: the movie *Something New*. I snagged the DVD from my sister. It's about an uptight African-American corporate woman and a carefree white gardener who are set up on a blind date, and even though they have beakers and beakers of chemistry, she's dead set on her ideal of a black man. Her friends tell her to "let go to let love flow." So she relinquishes all of her checklists and control, which is symbolized by letting her natural curly hair run loose and wearing flirty red dresses, and falls in love with the gardener. It's kind of cheesy but I actually take notes, jotting down the "let go" mantra in my mini notebook while Bart lies on his back, spread eagle, white belly fur exposed. Bart's not afraid to be vulnerable. Why should I be?

Jeannine is positive that my issue is not with any of the superficial problems I pluck from the men I date. It's with dating itself. "It should be *fun*," she told me. Meaning, I'm not having fun. Instead, I feel like an alien has jumped into my body and is wiggling around, moving organs, stretching muscles, trying to get settled in my skin, and I'm resisting it every step of the way.

The first step is to let go.

It's a beautiful day on the mountain. The sky is squeaky blue and the leaves are squeezing out the last of their green preparing to peak. Jen, Gabe, and I are scrambling over boulders at the top of Old Rag in Virginia, along with the rest of the D.C. metropolitan area (we actually had to wait in line to get past a few rock crevices). I got the idea for this hike on my last blind date set up by a college friend. It was actually my friend's friend, and while the once-removed lineage seemed like a dodgy proposition, and his phone voice indicated a fleshy former frat boy in a pink polo, I went because there wasn't a single other prospect. It had been a couple weeks since I'd been out with Lorenzo (with whom I was still exchanging emails), and even though this dating thing is supposed to mimic real life, I didn't have all the time in the world to be sitting around picking and choosing.

Pink wasn't fleshy, pink, or fratty. He was, however, buttoned up, and his hair was a study in calculated precision that only a black, fine-toothed pocket comb could create. A right-leaning politician's haircut. This shouldn't have been a surprise, since the friend who set us up is politically conservative and it would stand to reason that the pool of men she draws from might be, too, even though her last matchmaking attempt turned up a Vicodin-popping lawyer.

I had no idea which way Pink leaned politically. It didn't matter. I wasn't interested. He was a perfectly fine date and I had fun and could even imagine kissing him after a couple beers. But there wasn't enough chemistry to make me want to pursue another date with him. I, of course, didn't tell him that, and instead made an empty promise to go hiking.

I decided to go with my friends instead.

It was dark by the time I got home. Walking down the alley from my parking space, I felt the mid-October breeze carrying with it the first sign of winter. I'd need a coat the next day. It's always the day before I need to start wearing a coat that I remember The Ex. Actually, it's one memory that edges out all the rest and that sets the bar so high that no guy I've dated since has been able to slap it.

We'd been dating about two months and things had moved quickly. We snuck up to the top of the Washington Hotel on the service elevator one Saturday night after an Italian feast. The banquet room on the roof had a low buzz still dying from the night's party, and the white linens were damp with red splotches of spilled wine. On the balcony overlooking the Clinton-era White House, The Ex and I danced under the stars until the crisp breeze made me go in for a long hug, and we said I love you to each other for the first time. The words had been practically falling off my lips for weeks, and it was a relief to finally let them go and to know he felt the same way. And then we broke into a mad sprint racing from one end of the roof deck to the other because we were so goddamn excited. My neck and head felt like they were going to explode because there was one person in the world who felt about me the same way I felt about him. The stars marched in formation and I felt loved.

* * *

I made the shockingly huge mistake of getting my hair cut and highlighted three hours before meeting Lorenzo for our second date. I never like my hair right after a cut—or any other time for that matter. The problem is that the vision of what I want is long curls, preferably strawberry blond, which apparently isn't plausible without a perm when your hair is shoulder length, brown, and straight like mine.

"Can't you *cut* curls into my hair?" I asked my stylist.

She laughed. I wasn't joking.

Could it be this unreasonable approach to my hair (and often the rest of my physical appearance) is the same problem I have with my approach to men? If I don't accept myself as I am, how can I possibly begin to accept others for how they are? The answer is: I can't.

"Sorry I'm late." Lorenzo and I cheek kiss. It's familiar. It's nice. I've missed this feeling. I've met so many new people over the past four months and I always have to be "on." This feels comfortable.

He got his hair trimmed, too. It's way too short and he's breast-stroking in another billowy button-down and pleated pants. His clothes are way too big for him. He would be a good makeover project. I'd get him some tailored clothes, let the hair grow—I could chip away at his conservative exterior. It doesn't quite suit him as it is because he's only *fiscally* conservative (I verified this on our first date).

I sit across from him and there we are, face to face with our too-short hair.

"Are you sick?"

"Yeah. I've had this cold. . . ." I sneeze in confirmation. The flat note echoes in the serene harmony of Komi's Asian-inspired dining room.

"Well, don't try to kiss me at the end of the night or anything."

I'm not sure if he's kidding. He stumps me with his sarcasm, which he pulls off way too well. And I don't feel flirty, maybe because my head is stuffed to the gills with mucus.

The menu is a fixed multicourse menu with items like papardelle and suckling pig confit. Lorenzo had originally suggested a Smith & Wollensky–type joint, but I used the vegetarian excuse to finagle a quieter, more intimate spot that I would like. He looks intimidated by the menu, and probably feels like a Democrat standing in the voting booth at the 2004 elections. I unwittingly check off my cons list: Not adventurous with food.

Later, back at his very-male bachelor pad, he plays guitar and points rack up so quickly I can't keep count. All the grievances I've ever concocted about Lorenzo get sucked down the drain. Man plus guitar equals hot.

I'm draped over the arm of the couch, leaning in, listening, singing, and thinking, Maybe I *could* kiss him with mucus dripping down my nose. Lorenzo must sense he's about to get slimed and sets the guitar down.

"What? No more music?"

"Nah."

There we are. Sitting there. I sip my water. He doesn't seem to want to talk; we're clearly not going to make out. I take the hint. "Well, I guess I should go."

"Yeah? Okay. I'll walk you down." He's quick to agree.

He offers to pay for my cab home. No one has ever offered that before. I almost take him up on it because it seems novel and traditional. I don't, but I like that he wanted to make sure I got home safe.

Not-quite-rights should not make the cut.

"Your love life is in chaos right now, yes?" Miss Crystal, a psychic in Georgetown is reading my tarot. I'm on a mission to see five psychics in one day for a freelance assignment. Miss Crystal is number four.

"You will marry. An older man. Five to seven years older, in fact. I see you with two kids, but they are intertwined." She crosses her fingers and looks at me with her lazy eye. "Your husband will have the letter *J* in his name, but he's not in Washington." She fiddles with the ankh pendant dangling into her cleavage.

I smile helplessly. What am I supposed to do now? Move?

"The guys you're dating now are a waste of time because the man you'll marry is somewhere north, maybe Boston or New York City. And stay away from the dark-haired men. Go toward the lighter colors."

Then I meet Tina. She's the kind of psychic you find through word of mouth—through a friend of a friend's great-aunt's sister. I've never met her but she does a tarot card reading for me over the phone.

"You're listening to too many people. In your heart you know what you want to do, and know what will make you happiest, but fear is keeping you from doing that. You've been living inside your head lately, analyzing, and you haven't gotten out much. Is that right?"

"Yeah." Ruminations have commandeered my two-hour round-trip commute, my jogging time, and even some of my sleep time.

"You're seeing two men right now. Within the next year, you'll meet a man who brings you joy, love, and commitment. You will be indecisive, but just go for it. He's kind, wonderful, and joyful." She also says he'll be older and have brown hair. "Lots of people are telling you what to do, Rachel, but you have to go with your gut."

So I do. I decide I can't drag out things with Lorenzo and Pink if I'm not really into them, especially since there are mutual friends involved, who I'm partially worried will be mad at me if I handle things badly. I don't want to call either of them, so I start to craft a breakup email at work one afternoon. Fifteen minutes later, I'm still looking at a blank screen. I need some help. So I do what any thirty-three-year-old woman would do and ask my married boss to write the breakup email for me. This is what Mike sends:

Dear xxx,

I'm one of those people who likes to cut to the chase—and if that chase seems to meander through hills, valleys, and waterways, well, it's better not to waste anyone's time. And that, truth be told, is the crux of my dating life. Because you're such a great guy, I'd be truly bummed if I led you down a path that was going nowhere. I'm sorry! Hope this email finds you well. Thanks again for a lovely night . . .

I finesse it so it has my voice (and none of the waterways business) and send it to Pink. Select all, copy, paste in new email, change the name and send it to Lorenzo. I'm done in thirty seconds.

Now I brace myself for the replies. Pink's comes first. His note is short and sweet, thanking me for letting him know and to take care. Nice. Then Lorenzo's:

Yeah there didn't seem to be much spark, but I'm just trying to get to know you. Let's be friends!

Really? He didn't feel a spark? I mean, I know I didn't feel much of a spark, but that doesn't mean I don't want him to feel a spark.

A blind-date dry spell is spilling over into its fourth week. I'm bored. I was up to my ears with dating, but now that there are no prospects, no crushes, I feel a little lost. There's nothing to look forward to, so I activate my profile on the Onion and have my mom sign up on MatchmakingMoms.com, a website I'd heard about where moms put up profiles of their kids and search for a match for them. If she finds one she likes, she contacts the other mom and arranges a date. I lead her through the profile process because it will never get done if I don't. This inevitably leads to an argument.

"Eye color, green." I hear her clicking on the drop-down menu item.

"My eyes are blue." Irritated. I'm irritated.

"Well, they turn green sometimes."

"Sometimes they may appear green when I cry." Which I'm about to do right now.

"Weellll . . ." My mother says this as if she's proved a valid point.

I'm silent.

"Okay. Blue. Height, five foot ten."

"Stop!"

"All the guys lie about their height! You might as well, too." She's indignant as she continues the profile of lies. "Religion, Catholic."

I throw my head back on my chair. "Okay. Seriously. Just stop. Do you even know me? I have blue eyes, I am five eight and a half, and I haven't willingly gone to church, ever." I think I can officially quit therapy now, having uncovered the source of my fantastical thinking that leads to unrealistic expectations.

We get through filling out the profile that mildly represents who I am, and after all of that hassle, there's one guy who comes up in search results for the immediate D.C. area. *One* guy with a Jewish mother who most certainly would not want a shiksa as a daughter-in-law.

On a gray Saturday in November, I have nothing to do. Actually, I was supposed to meet the newish neighbor, Trey. Kenneth had been bugging me about how hot he was and how I *had* to meet him. "You're gonna think he is so hot. So. Hot. You have to have sex with him. And I want to watch."

I rolled my eyes. The last time Kenneth facilitated a date for me, I ended up at a creepy dance club with my date (also a neighbor) and his coworkers from a local hair salon. My date got lost in the crowd and I ended up dancing all night with the shampoo guy, who was also the dishwasher at the neighboring French café.

I got up early anyway to make chocolate chip cookies for Trey, but when Kenneth and I knocked on his door, he was a no-show. So I ate every last cookie between two fifteen and eight p.m. while cleaning my apartment and dancing around to Pat Benatar.

By nine, I'm on the couch, sick to my stomach. This is when Ethan texts me to meet at Tryst. I jump. If it were anyone else, I probably would have said no. But for some reason, I can't say no to Ethan. We've known each other a long time—ever since he was two feet shorter than me and I had a crush on him anyway—and have circulated in and out of each other's lives for many years.

Ethan is sort of an ambiguous friend. Ambiguous because we've made out a couple of times and it's suspect if a man and a woman can truly just be friends. I've had mild success with the notion. I can honestly and positively say that there's no ambiguity with my friend Patrick. We don't have the emotional push and pull resulting from one person or the other wanting more.

The push and pull did exist with Ethan, though—at least for me—and, at one point, those forces distorted the boundaries of our friendship so that we ended up in the confusing predicament of acting like an old married couple: supper together, TV in silence, sleepovers—but nothing physical. And then, after a few months, we crossed over the invisible boundary. I finally pushed too hard and forced an awkward drunken conversation at three a.m. about what was happening between the two of us. I was confused, because there's always been a part of me that wanted more from him, but he was always busy dating someone else. I suppose I figured it was finally my turn and it seemed like we were almost there. He played some song to explain to me how he felt about our relationship, but I couldn't make out a single lyric. To this day, I still don't know what song he played. I just assumed if there was a song about it, he wanted more. He didn't. I thought I did. I felt like an idiot. We didn't talk for a year.

We finally moved past the awkwardness and now, even though I still feel the push and pull, I know my boundaries, even if I do want to leap over them sometimes.

"Wanna share a waffle?" Ethan smiles at me. He has the kind of smile that makes me feel like I'm the only one in the room. I always wonder if he feels the same chemistry that I do.

I lie to be easy even though my stomach is still churning from the cookies. "Sure, a waffle would be good."

We sink into a ratty coffeehouse love seat, sitting close together and talking about the future and ideas and life for hours while eating a Belgian waffle with Nutella and strawberries. It's so cozy and cuddly, but when I come back from a trip to the bathroom, the dynamic is all out of whack. Ethan is chatting up a couple sitting near us, who, actually, is not a couple. They're medical students in town for a conference.

"So are *you* guys together?" Boy Doc is asking.

Ethan and I laugh without looking at each other and say no. And even though we're joking about how the doctors are trolling for a place to crash, I'm certain there isn't any real chemistry between any of us. I'm so naïve.

At some point during the night, there's a couple swap that anyone with only one good eye and the hearing capacity of CarrotTop could have predicted. Not me. I'm so confident and firm in my belief that it's still my night out with Ethan that I feel like I've been punched in the stomach when he swings his arm around Girl Doc outside of Tryst and leads her down the street toward his place with a toothy grin on his face. "Guess we'll see you guys later."

My head swirls. What just happened? I stand helpless on the sidewalk among the herd of drunken goats milling around with enormous slices of pizza melting over cardboard boxes.

I look at Boy Doc. I look down the sidewalk, where the goats swallow up Ethan and Girl Doc. I look back at Boy Doc. "Guess you're coming with me."

This was probably one of those situations where I should have shoved Boy Doc in a cab and sent him on his way. But I didn't.

Ethan called me the next morning after I dropped Boy Doc off. I was upset with him for ditching me and waiting so long to see if I was okay. What if Boy Doc had turned out to be a crazy psycho and not the smart, interesting, and brilliant kisser I discovered he was? I made Ethan apologize and promise never to leave me like that again, and then we didn't talk for at least a month because that's how our relationship goes.

Wait for it, and chemistry will eventually make a showing.

Dinner? Tonight?

The text message sends me into a fit of excitement. It's from Justin Timberframe. I met him under the unlikeliest of circumstances—at the Timber Framers Guild conference. I go to this conference for work twice a year and it's always packed with long-haired hippies in flannels, denim, and suspenders who look fresh from spending time outdoors in nature. I like these people. They're salt of the earth and remind me of what's good and simple in life.

This time though, there's Justin Timberframe. He's single, my age, tall, and has the cutest Boston accent. And we have amazing chemistry. Heart palpitating, weak-kneed chemistry.[5]

He was passing through town for the night and catching a flight the next morning. He wanted to get together. That's all I needed to hear. I drove straight down to the Metro station to pick him up that evening.

Prickly rain falls through the layer of humidity left over from the unseasonably hot weekend and we race into Busboys

---

[5] The chemistry cocktail: phenylethylamine (speeds up information flow between cells), dopamine (makes you feel all glowy), and norepinephrine (stimulates the adrenaline). These chemicals are addictive—making the person who's causing the reaction an addiction. Like crack cocaine. These chemicals are responsible for wars and misery.

and Poets, a café and bookstore with a low, heavy buzz that soothes.

Justin Timberframe looks at me over his baked salmon. He's wearing a Red Sox cap and a fleece, the same outfit he wore all weekend at the conference. It's cute. "So this is kind of our second date."

"Actually, it's our first date." I won't purport to be a dating expert, but this much I know. We'd gone out for drinks one evening with a few of his coworkers, and while it was mostly Justin Timberframe and me close talking over Amstel Lights, it was not a date. "You can't count Friday night as a date. We weren't even alone. You didn't ask me out." We smile at each other and a hot flash prickles my skin under my heavy cowl neck.

During the part of our conversation about the book he's reading on decoding body language, I realize how I've been sitting. Normally, I lean back in my chair with my arms crossed in front of me, as emotionally and mentally unavailable as it gets—or perhaps I'm just cold. Here, both of my hands grip either end of the table and I'm leaning into the space between us as if I'm about to address an audience from a pulpit.

I back off from my position slowly on the off chance he didn't notice that I was showing him my entire mental and emotional hand.

Or maybe this window into how I'm feeling with him is a good thing because we graduate from his holding the small of my back as we walk out of the restaurant to his taking my hand as we run across the street in the rain to another bar for a nightcap, to his holding on to my knee while we sit across from each other talking about the only thing we have in common: our chemistry. There's a lot to talk about. Who felt what when, why he didn't notice me trying to get his attention at first, apologies that he didn't notice. We hash out our first meeting as if we'd been dating for months instead of only knowing each other for three days. By one a.m., there's nothing more to say, so I drive him to where he's staying.

He's looking at me sideways in the passenger seat while my car idles in the rain. "You could stay over." My pupils have to be the size of Kalamata olives. We're going to kiss. And we do. It's sweet and gentle and soft and he touches my jaw and my cheek and my hair and lingers at my lips. He doesn't ruin it with a mouth full of tongue or a boob grab. It's exactly how it should be.

"I'm not sure how to leave things." He puts his hand on my leg. "But let's stay in touch." He squeezes my knee and gets out in the rain. He's gone.

There's a final text on my ride home.

night Rachel

I'm intoxicated with the possibility of him. I let my fantasizing run wild. I imagine my wedding dress—simple, crisp, and white this time, and I put my first name with his last name even though I would never change my name in real life. I consider what it would be like to move—to live near him. I'm way too far ahead of myself, but it's fun to be preoccupied. My spine is tingling; my head is buzzing, and my eyes spring open at six a.m. the next morning. It's been many moons since I felt this level of chemistry.

Now that I've felt a real spark, it's apparent to me how trace (or nonexistent) the chemistry was with all the other guys I've been out with lately. I'd been trying to coerce myself into liking someone, to give everyone a chance, to manufacture a spark out of a pile of damp leaves. It's been so long since I've truly felt moved by a single man that I doubted my ability to know if I really liked someone. I gloss over the fundamental issue that Justin Timberframe lives ten hours away, because that's what happens when groovy chemicals are injected into your brain. They make you put practicality aside and allow yourself to be washed over in a glow that, let's face it, makes you a little dumb. So dumb, the wheels are already turning in my head about how I can make this thing with him work, which wouldn't be such a terrible thing if maybe Justin Timberframe and I had talked about it and it was something he wanted, too.

If this weren't enough to keep me busy, a week later I tap into more chemistry. I'm awash with chemicals. I can barely see straight.

I meet The Gentle Artist on the Onion. He's "intrigued" by my smile. He's an artist. He's tall. He lives in my area code. We'd been emailing for two days when he spontaneously invites me to Cirque du Soleil.

Come to the circus with me!

My heart is a flying trapeze. But it's Wednesday. I have therapy on Wednesdays. I call and lie to Judith about why I'm not coming. This is bad. There are a multitude of problems involved with lying to your therapist. But Judith makes it tough to cancel.

If she didn't, people would cancel all the time because going to therapy is hard work.

But The Gentle Artist. He's so lovely with his warm smile, a delicious gap between his front teeth, and a muted pompadour. His hug hello felt like he'd been practicing warm embraces as often as I stare at my ass in the mirror. He's better than I could have ever imagined. Not only is there chemistry, I feel like we "fit." I like the way he sounds and looks and what he says and his way with people. Confident but not overbearing—sure of himself.

The circus is the perfect date; maybe even better than Frisbee. Our arms and legs brush and rest near each other and we steal sidelong glances and get lost in the fantasy of bendy gymnasts in pantaloons manipulating themselves around gigantic chandeliers twenty feet up, bicycles riding on the air, and midgets bobbing above the audience like a beach ball at a Phish concert.

"Is the night over?" The Gentle Artist looks expectant as we stand facing each other outside the big tents after the show.

I'm exhausted and have been stifling yawns for an hour. But I don't want the night to end. I know there's something to quitting while you're ahead, but the fact that neither of us want to leave trumps any sort of dating wisdom. So what if I have to slap my face to stay awake through a strawberry margarita?

It's a useless hour of basking in the company of this cuddly stranger who completely abuses his right to concoct hybrid words culled from every sentence we utter: strawgerita, midgetastic, circolay. It's annoying, but his hair is so thick and brown. I want to run my fingers through it.

I sit close to The Gentle Artist on the Metro ride home. We ran out of things to talk about ten minutes ago and I fade into the late hour. I lean in closer to him, pretending we're a couple. At my stop, he confirms our original plan to have Thanksgiving morning Bloody Marys the following week. I recite my number as he keys it into his cell. We hug good-bye. He kisses my cheek. "Mmmmm." He murmurs soft and low, like a cat getting a chin rub.

I never see him again. Instead, I get an email after five days:

i am newly returned to the dating pool. And i am just putting my foot in to test the waters, but i am still unsure of the wisdom of fully submerging. I enjoyed hanging out with you, and i look forward to hanging out again, but i think I need to keep on a slow and non-physical pace right now. I thought that you should know that because maybe you are looking for something more immediately romantic, and better to be honest with you, and myself, that I am not ready for that.

Now it's clear to me why he was so comfortable and familiar. He's still in relationship mode. He's used to being that way with a woman. He puts it to me to come up with our next "hangout," and that's when I knew it would never be. A man without a plan is an uninterested man. This doesn't stop me from sending a desperate email two weeks later when I never hear from him under the guise that maybe there was a technical failure. The only failure, though, is my inability to recognize someone who doesn't want to date me, even though that's exactly what he's telling me. It's amazing the untruths we can talk ourselves into. But I didn't want to hear the truth, because it seems that the truth is always disappointing.

Disappointment is part of the process, though, and just might be an indicator that the person disappointing you isn't the one you should be with. That's how Nan sees it, at least. Nan is a former coworker. Even though there's a fifteen-year age difference between us and our lives are worlds apart, we get each other, and when we meet for lunch every month or so, I tell her about my dating life and she offers bits of wisdom about how love should be. It's never a sugarcoated fairy tale, but rather snippets of Midwestern practicality that somehow sound romantic in her flat and nasal delivery.

On disappointment: "You know how I knew Gene was the one? He never disappointed me. That's how you know you've found a good one. He won't ever disappoint you."

I believe this, but what constitutes disappointment? Don't expectations have to be rational to properly assess disappointment? Disappointment seems to be a common thread in my dating relationships. But I'm not willing to point the guilty finger at every single guy who has disappointed me, because, lately, that's everyone. I'm disappointed by hair, kissing technique, height, restaurant picks. I'm the common denominator in all of these star-crossed affairs, and I can't start casting off men based on my unrealistic expectations.

All of a sudden, it was Christmas. Unlike years past, my dance card was filled with holiday parties and men. I was starting to confuse men, and not just the men I was involved with. The backlog of names was catching up with me. I finally took to skipping first names when addressing any male for fear of uttering the wrong one.

Normally I'd be stressed over maintaining this web of suitors. But I'm energized and a little smug about it. It's the holidays, after all, and I feel entitled to the attention. The last few Decembers were lonely and I'd start thinking about the fact that I'm not in love (or in like) with anyone enough to exchange gifts with in the glow of tree lights and Bing Crosby. I wanted the holidays to pass quickly and quietly, like an early morning dusting of snow that melts before noon.

This year was different. I'd had the revelation driving home from work one day that I am actually happy with my life. That I actually don't want to be married with kids right now. For so long, I'd been feeling like the odd one out—always the bridesmaid, the auntie, the single friend. But I realized I'm the only one making myself feel that way. My life as it is, is as it should be. I was at peace with myself and the world around me. The feeling is usually fleeting, but it's wonderful when it's happening.

I had a few men keeping me busy after all: late-night pillow talks with Justin Timberframe; emails with Lorenzo, who was wiggling back into the picture even though I'd cast him out; calls from a random guy I gave my number to at a Thievery Corporation concert who eventually fizzled; and GOP.

GOP was another blind date. We met at Asylum, a motorcycle bar that serves vegan food, and I talked and talked and talked. I've never talked so much on a date in my entire life. I found myself telling him thoughts and feelings I don't share with anyone. He had everything I could and should ever want in a guy—he's easy to talk to, has confidence, has a good job, dresses well, owns a home, is smart, likes gadgets, can rewire electrical. I called him GOP not because he's a Republican, but because he's good on paper. Yet I didn't know if I wanted to kiss him. Surely there had to be *something* there if I was that comfortable with him.

So I took another stab and asked out GOP for a lunch date. I thought meeting in the afternoon would take the pressure off. It would be casual, light and easy. No decisions would have to be made.

On a rainy Friday afternoon three days before Christmas, I pick up GOP for a late lunch at a British pub. We're in heavy sweaters and jeans, and icy rain is beating at the window by the street while we drink hot buttered rums by the fireplace. It doesn't get much more intimate, and I'm sure this is the way to find that spark with GOP. But the match won't strike. In fact, the matchbook is empty. I can't create the physical chemistry.

Know what can, though? Sierra Nevada Pale Ale. I had several at GOP's house when I'd dropped him off and he invited me in for a tour of his place. It was meant to be a five-minute tour. Ten minutes, tops. I had every intention of going to a yoga class and to bed early. I'd joined the Studio Serenity above the Subway and was making a concerted effort to be more balanced, healthier, and serene, and not to drink so much because my toxicity levels were at an all-time high. I was living my life according to dating, which seemed to go hand in hand with drinking.

Instead of yoga, though, I hang out with GOP on his futon, listening to a French songbird trill through his fancy sound system. We drink and drink and talk and drink some more (so much for laying off the drinks). I'm halfway through my fifth beer and officially tanked when I pull out from under our blanket cocoon to go to the bathroom. My bladder is about to burst, and when I teeter to sit on GOP's brand-new Kohler porcelain toilet seat, I'm so intent on relief, I forget to slowly release in order to diffuse the gasses that have built up from the mass quantity of carbonation, barley, and hops I've consumed.

I'm horrified by how loud I fart. Noxious gas that sounds like it's been pent up for centuries explodes in the echo chamber that is the basement bathroom. I sit there on the pristine toilet seat and consider that maybe he didn't hear it. I wait. And wait. But not too long, because then he'll think I'm not just peeing—that perhaps I have explosive diarrhea.

I weigh my options. There's the comic approach: Walk out laughing and say something like, "Did you hear that thunder outside?" The honest approach: Walk out with both hands on my stomach and complain of feeling gassy. The coward approach: Squeeze through the mini window at the top of the wall that most definitely leads into a drug-deal zone in the alley behind his house. I opt for option four, and go back and sit on the couch, pretending nothing happened. And I was so drunk that by three minutes later, it actually might not have.

Maybe GOP didn't hear, because he kisses me. And then, he's up from the couch with the intent to mobilize to a more advantageous spot. We just started kissing. It's only our second date. These concerns backstroke lazily through the alcohol drowning my judgment. I take his hand and he leads me to the bedroom.

Even in an alcohol-induced passion, I know creating a false sense of intimacy through premature sexual relations does not a relationship make. And when I wake up the next morning with a vomitous headache, I'm thankful for this bit of wisdom that squeezed through all that beer. Nonetheless, there seems to be the morning cuddle to contend with, and I can't get out of there fast enough. "Shit! I gotta go! I'm supposed to meet my friend for brunch!" It's a lie, but I can't deal with faking feelings. I go home and spoon with Bart because the only friskiness he'll expect is out of a can.

I wake up four hours later as if it's a new day, the night before but a dream I remember in fits and stops. A text comes in. It's Lorenzo.

busy tonight?

I stare at the question on my phone. *Am* I busy tonight? It's the night before Christmas Eve, all of my friends are out of town and the one person I'm dating I ran away from. Nope. I'm not busy. And I'm strangely not hungover anymore.

Me: nope.
L: want to go to a party?
Me: sure

Rejection is a gift in the end (even if they don't always pick up on it).

"So how long have you two been together?" The buxom blonde with the bloodred lips and the tight black cocktail dress smiles too widely at Lorenzo and me. I look at Lorenzo in his oversized collared shirt and khakis. He's so preppy and cute. Now that we're friends, I don't have any unfair expectations of him. He doesn't flinch and tells her casually that we're friends. I want to hug him for being so cool. But were we just friends? I'd been wondering what he'd been thinking ever since we met before the party and he paid for my drinks. I couldn't tell if he was trying to be brotherly or if he was vying for the possibility of more. I wasn't sure how I felt, either, though I'd gotten ready as if it were a date. I even curled my hair and switched the gray sweater I'd been wearing all month for a fluttery low-cut top.

As we stand there chatting, a guy who I'd been out with two years before arrives. James. We'd met online. I remember him talking the whole time on our date and not seeming interested in me at all. We emailed a little after that, but then I stopped hearing from him. I think. Or maybe I stopped emailing. When we're introduced, I look for a flicker of recognition. Nothing. Really? How could he not remember me? Maybe he does and is pretending he doesn't, like I am.

I spend the next hour avoiding James, because even though any memory of me seems lost on him, one conversation about where I work, which will inevitably come up because that's what people talk about at parties, will tip him off. People may not comprehend *Log Home Living* at first, but they don't forget it. I don't even consider why it matters if he figures out that we went out one time. I just know I'd be embarrassed.

I stick close to Lorenzo in the doorway of the kitchen while he fields the questions that everyone seems to have about our marital status. A faceless arm extends from the kitchen to offer me a second Pisco Sour. I accept greedily. I need all the Pisco I can get.

Three Sours and one terrible lie later—about being a research scientist to avoid talking about my job in front of James so there's no chance he will ever remember our date—I give up the charade and corner him on the couch. "You know . . . we went out once."

He studies my face. His is blank.

I jog his memory. "Met on the Onion a couple years ago . . . drinks at Chief Ike's . . ."

Still blank. Do I look *that* different?

His amnesia rights itself. "Editor, yes, Blelvis sang for us." Blelvis! I forgot about black Elvis, a homeless guy who used to roam my neighborhood singing his renditions of Elvis songs—and pretty darn well. He'd stopped at our table on the patio at Chief Ike's Mambo Room and sang "Love Me Tender," for which he demanded a cigarette and/or money as payment. I think I poured some of my beer into his cup and he walked away bellowing, "and my darlin', I love yooooooo, and I allllll-waaaaays wiiiiilllll."

"Yep. That was me."

He smiles and sighs. "How come we never went out again?"

Because you never asked. "Oh. I don't know. It was so long ago . . ."

He seems so different now. He's more relaxed. Maybe I'm more relaxed. Maybe because we're not on a date, we can be more relaxed and not give in to expectations. However, it could also be timing. Our date was two years ago. People change. I probably wasn't ready for anything more than our one date, coming out of my Saturn Return and all. It wouldn't have mattered how or where we met. But maybe I was too quick to dismiss him and I should have pressed for a second date.

When I say good night to James, telling him I know where to find him when he reiterates that we should hang out, I know I won't contact him. Right now, I have enough ambiguous friends, and one, it seems, is about to walk me home.

"I'm gonna come up to meet Bart."

It's two thirty in the morning and I wonder what Lorenzo is really thinking. Is he spinning a web? Am I about to get trapped? But like the night before, caution has taken a dip into some seriously inebriated gray matter. In retrospect, it seems incredibly naive to have questioned whether a man who has walked me home and invited himself up to my apartment in the wee hours is interested in anything but making out. But I really don't get it. I genuinely think he's here for the cat, so when Lorenzo dives across the couch for a kiss, I'm stunned. But then, he's a fantastic kisser, so I wouldn't want to waste that. It falls apart quickly though. He goes to the bathroom to pee or check condom status or pop a zit, and I dive in my bed facedown because all the drinking and late nights are catching up with me. My thought process is this: He will come out of the bathroom, crawl into my bed and spoon me, fully clothed on top of the covers. It sounds so nice and cozy. Instead, he walks out of the bathroom, takes one look at his window of opportunity that violently slammed shut while he was away, and hightails it out of my apartment faster than I left GOP's house.

One concern trails through the last fired synapse of the night as I pass out alone with a cat head butting me: He's mad.

He's not mad. Lorenzo is the first to text me a Merry Christmas! I get two more messages that morning. The second is from an ex-boyfriend who, since our breakup more than five years ago, has popped up about once every six months to check in. The third is from GOP. I'm definitely not alone this holiday. But for some reason, the attention from the not-quite-rights makes me tired because I feel the weight of their expectation that I've fabricated in my head. Everything makes me tired. Hanging out with friends on Christmas night for Jen's birthday makes me tired. I haven't been out *not* on a date (or with someone wondering if it was a date) in weeks. I'm surrounded by friends and people who could be friends, but I still feel lonely and guilty because I feel this way. All that self-assurance about everything being as it should be in my life has disappeared.

On New Year's I decide to hang out with the only guy in my life I'm sure about: Ethan. Actually, I'm not that sure about him, but I do feel comfortable with him. He's part of my security blanket and I always seem to make my way back to his familiar smell and warm hugs that disguise the ambiguity and question marks that define our time together. Besides, we'd promised each other a couple months before that we'd spend New Year's together. Since then, he had started dating someone that he even says might be The One. But she lives in another city, so as far as I'm concerned, she doesn't exist. Jugs of Italian wine, bottomless flutes of champagne, and one well-placed party hat that I inscribed with the words "Kiss me, I'm not at all particular" set the stage for the evening.

There's a halfhearted countdown to midnight and Ethan and I kiss cheeks. I'm disappointed. I don't know why since *he's dating someone else*. Nonetheless, twenty minutes later, I stand within inches of his face, say something unintelligible, and, lost to the drunken swim team in my head, kiss him on the lips.

"Why are you kissing me like that?" He's surprised but he's smiling.

Even though I shouldn't have pursued Ethan that night because he is unavailable to me and we will never be in a dating relationship, I didn't care. I didn't expect anything from him, and better yet, I realized I didn't *want* anything from him. And I *am* particular. It was like a switch flipped in my head and all of a sudden I saw the control board for my life just sitting there unmanned, waiting for me to hop on board and start steering. I felt empowered and it made me want to start fixing things. I hadn't had a good New Year's resolution in a while, so this year I came up with two: Be more upfront with people and trust my instincts. I start with GOP, whom I call a few days later to make the break.

"I think I need to be friends." I squint my eyes and brace myself for the pain. One hand holds my cell phone to my ear while the other fist pierces the air above my head, which had been burrowing under my armpit, ready for the blow. I'd decided it wasn't going to work after throwing GOP into the mix with my friends one night and realizing that while I could fake it when it was only the two of us, once you start the socialization process as a couple, there's no hiding a bad fit.

I'd been agonizing over telling him how I was feeling. No one likes rejection, but I have an overwhelming fear of it. Not necessarily getting rejected, though that smarts, too. It's mostly a fear of handing out rejection. Being the rejector. I will do just about anything to avoid confrontation and being the bad guy, because I'm afraid of the backlash. I suppose I've been avoiding getting involved with someone so I wouldn't have to be in this situation where more is involved than a couple of casual dates. Yet here I am.

It's quiet. "Oh . . ." He doesn't sound upset. Just thoughtful and surprised. But he's okay. I'm lighthearted to the point of being annoyingly smug. Saying how I feel and getting a positive result is so satisfying and freeing. Knowing that I'm capable of calling it quits with men ironically makes it easier for me to want to get involved with them.

It's becoming quite clear that I am not attracted to men who have any sort of potential for a relationship. I've found something wrong with all of the men who are interested in me and live within five miles. However, get me near someone who isn't interested, is vaguely interested, or is interested but who lives in another state, and I'll voluntarily rip my heart out of my chest and set it on the ground to be stomped on.

As far as blind dating goes, having my friends set me up, if nothing else, made me slow down. It slowed me down so much I ended up having to do some work to keep the dating wheels turning lest I lose momentum and abort the whole mission.

Naturally, the efficacy of blind dating is determined by how many people you know who are capable of and willing to set you up. I had friends mention possible dates but not follow through. People are busy and have jobs and kids and lives, and my dating life was not a top priority for them. It can only be a top priority for me. Which is why blind dating seems like more of a supplemental dating approach.

However, the men I went out with on blind dates seemed to be closer fits. Even though I spent most of my time uncovering the things I didn't like about them, I still found a level of familiarity that I partially attribute to being from similar social networks. It's not so far-fetched to think that since friends are a reflection of aspects of our personalities, it would stand to reason that one of their friends could be a good match. I may not have hit the bull's-eye this time, but it felt like my darts weren't flying at random anymore.

Chemistry is still the elusive X factor. I'd finally found some, and it was an important step (I was seriously beginning to doubt myself) because now I can confidently identify when chemistry *isn't* there so I don't have to brutalize myself with endless dates because I'm not sure.

This will come in handy for my next charge: professional matchmakers. I will pit human against machine. Contenders are It's Just Lunch, which, in my opinion, charges a high-enough fee that they should be able to create chemistry out of thin air, versus eHarmony, which promises a no-fail matching method with machine-run personality tests and the power of science. I'm dubious about both, but my mind is open.

Matchmakers

A Lesson in the Business of Love

PART I: IT'S JUST LUNCH

Now that I'll be paying for services rendered and not just relying on friends with their own lives and kids to raise, I have a mountain of expectations for my matchmakers. For instance, when I go to plunk down my $1,300 for a year and/or fourteen dates at the It's Just Lunch (IJL) offices downtown, I'm expecting a spa environment with celery-colored walls, bamboo plants, maybe a water element, and of course a glass of white wine. What I get is an empty sterile room and a paper cup of water.

The idea with IJL is that a lunch (or brunch or drinks) date is the ideal date. It's noncommittal—you're in, you're out—and the company credits themselves with 30,000 clients nationwide and are "responsible for over two million fun first dates."

I'd already had a phone interview with one of the counselors to establish what kind of man I'm looking for and if they had any clients who matched that. This second interview was to see if I'm a "fit" for the company, which, in my opinion, I'm not because I'm not too busy with a high-powered job to arrange my own social life, and the thought of meeting someone who is bothers me. I don't like the idea of people doing things for me that I can very well do on my own, even if I do a shitty job of it. Cleaning house, setting up dates—these are things I'm capable of. (I make exceptions for the occasional mani/pedi, of course.)

I filled out a questionnaire that read like an online profile and, as I was instructed by my intake counselor, Kiki, produced a list of the qualities that, for me, make up the perfect guy. I scribbled down said list right before my appointment: tall, dark hair, ridiculously confident, genuine, smiley, dry wit, clever, devastatingly smart, happy with where he is in life, loves his family, has a job, creative in some way, fit but not a gym rat, open to new things. Kiki, a high-strung bird with an eye for Ann Taylor Loft, and I chatted like old girlfriends about my past relationships and more on what I was looking for. It was fun to talk about me, me, me, and have someone so invested in my dating life. Even if I had to pay for it.

She jotted down everything I said in a file and told me she would come up with three or four descriptor words like "smart," "down-to-earth," and "charming," that other counselors would use to describe me to potential matches. I want to ask her what my descriptors are, but I feel like this information is off limits.

"I can already think of two guys who will be perfect for you!"

She smiles with her teeth, not her eyes. "Once we get you processed, we can get started right away!"

Right away means two weeks later. And then, one morning at work, she calls. "Hey, Rachel! It's Kiki at IJL!" She pronounces it in Valley Girl–ese as *eye-jay-ahlle*. "I have a match and I want to go over him with you!"

I pull out my yellow sticky pad, pencil at the ready.

"He's a CPA, thirty-five, no kids, six feet tall with hazel/brown eyes. He loves running and working out. Here's a fun little tidbit: He has a collection of more than fifteen hundred CDs! The words his counselor used to describe him are fun, caring, honest, and overall good guy!"

Breathe, Kiki, breathe.

"Sounds great!" I talk in exclamation points, too.

I mean it, though I also think that "no" would not be an acceptable response here.

Dating as semi-blindfolded target practice.

As I approach the annoyed staff behind the host podium at Zaytinya, a swanky restaurant in Penn Quarter, I look around to make sure no one is listening. I'd been dreading this moment since getting on the Metro. My expectation for having a matchmaker was that I'd have someone to handhold me through the dating process. You'd think I'd have my expectations in check by now. But for me, $1,300 is a small fortune, so it's hard not to want everything to be laced in gold with a red carpet rollout and maybe even a personal umbrella handler thrown into the mix, too. This is not the case. I'm totally on my own, and while IJL did set up the date, I still have to announce myself to the host.

"Hey. I'm Rachel from IJL?" I speak in a high-pitched whisper. This might be more stigmatizing than dating online. There's a blank look from the girl with curlicue locks. But then she turns all business. I search her face for an indicator of who I'll be meeting. Does she wince? Grimace? Smile? But there's nothing. I follow her into the bar area packed with posturing Washingtonians and we stop at the pasty guy with the glasses standing alone—the one I was hoping we would march right by. This was my date.

As I throw back a gin gimlet with CPA Man, I wonder what about my interview with Kiki made her think we'd be good together. There was never going to be a spark with this guy; physically, socially, it wasn't there. It would never be there. Didn't I say creative streak, some edge, looks are *somewhat* important? I want to shake the exclamation points out of Kiki and yell, "Would *you* date him?"

I consider exiting after forty-five minutes. It's just drinks, after all. There's no reason to stick it out. But I stay. Even though 110 percent of my being knows this is going nowhere, I continue the date because I don't want to hurt CPA Man's feelings. It's not a terrible date. He's a solid guy. But I'm not attracted to him. He doesn't have any confidence, and he hates his job. I've hated enough jobs to know that trying to date someone who isn't doing what he loves—or even likes—can be trying. We struggle to find something in common, which tonight seems to be that we're both on our first date with IJL.

For some inexplicable reason, I take CPA Man's card and agree that we should get together again. I'd forgotten what Kiki told me to say when I wasn't interested in someone. Something about "good luck with IJL." Maybe Kiki can tell him I'm not interested. Isn't that what she's paid to do? The answer to this is no, she's not paid to do anything except set me up. For some reason, I even thought IJL paid for the dates because their service is so pricey. Not that either. The entire time I worked with IJL, I wondered what exactly I was paying for because it sure felt like their process for making matches wasn't much different from my friends'.

I call IJL two days later for my debriefing. I was supposed to touch base the morning after the date, but I avoided it as I would have avoided breaking it off with someone. Even telling a go-between I'm not interested and the reasons why is tough for me. I'm worried they will be mad and I will be in trouble for not being a more cooperative client and not going ahead and marrying CPA Man to make everyone's job easier. Kiki isn't there, so I talk to Lulu, another counselor who also speaks in exclamation points. I wonder how this will work since Kiki is my handler and she supposedly *knows* me and my personal preferences.

I end up being more forgiving about my date than I had planned because it wasn't Lulu who actually set me up. Technically, the bad match wasn't her fault. I'm tactful about my disappointment because I don't want her to be turned off and set me up with worse matches. Must keep my eye on the prize.

But I'm honest, and say physically, no, the rest of it, no. And I explain myself: "He's really nice, but a little stuffy. And I think I need to up the looks quotient."[6] And to temper all of my superficiality: "But he really is *so nice.*"

I console myself with Justin Timberframe, who has lost only a little cachet because he's five states away. In some ways, I like the distance. There's no pressure to do or be anything. His presence is like background music that I can turn up whenever I feel like it, and we email and text consistently. And sometimes we talk on the phone. He verbally leads me around his apartment, and I tell him what brand of toothpaste I use. We argue over the best body products and compare reading lists. I'm so caught up in the novelty of our special get-to-know-you process that it doesn't occur to me how absurd it is, especially since we never seem to discuss the fact that we don't live in the same city. There's a physical and emotional distance that I pretend that I want to bridge, but really, if Justin Timberframe were here right now, would I find him so appealing?

In any case, I did want to see him again, so when I started planning a trip to New York City for my first attempt at dating in other cities, I told him if he could get down there, I'd make out with him in Central Park. I was half kidding; mostly thinking he wouldn't take the dare.

His response: *What days?*

---

[6] IJL offers three options for looks: not important, somewhat important, and very important. Initially, I chose "somewhat important," so if this is it, I'll need to upgrade.

* * *

Three days after CPA Man, Lulu calls with my second date. I guess Kiki and I are over. "I've got a great new match for you! He's Pakistani and Italian, so dark hair and hazel eyes. He's six foot three and a portfolio manager who is active with golf and tennis, loves music, poetry, art, and plays the guitar. His counselor describes him as intellectual, generous with a nice outlook." A Renaissance man.

Even though we've never met and she doesn't know me from a hole in the wall, maybe Lulu did get it. Ren Man on paper at least, is my type.

"We're thinking Sunday evening at six in Arlington. We picked Harry's Tap Room because it's a little closer to him."

I can't think of a worse day, time, or location (more than three blocks away) to have a date. But this is about opportunity. I must be open to opportunity at all times of day and night. Let go. Let flow.

Yeah. No.

Two strikes for IJL.

I call for my debriefing the next morning and brace myself for an angry woman on the other end of the line when I tell her Ren Man isn't quite right. I can hear Lulu saying, "We ask that you keep an open mind." But I don't get Lulu when I call. I get Buffy. "Hey, Rachel! Lulu's out of the office today, so you can chat with me!" Too many men, too many matchmakers. I can't keep everyone straight and I doubt very much my little cheerleading squad at IJL can either. "How was the date last night?"

"Oh, you know. He was *very* nice. Definitely getting closer. Very handsome, he's creative, loves his family, very outgoing." I list all of his positive attributes that actually fit the criteria I gave them about the men I want to date, but there were deal breakers, too, starting with the fact that he lived thirty miles away, and insisted on having the date closer to him. Ren Man also did not let me get a word in edgewise. Even when he asked me questions, he'd turn it back on himself and then comment that I was quiet. I don't report on this, though, because I don't think it will matter. It's not like they're going to change his profile so that when someone from IJL calls his next potential date she says, "The words his counselor used to describe him are intellectual, generous, nice outlook, but just so you know, he *really* likes talking about himself."

"I guess there wasn't much of a spark."

"Yeah . . . there's not much we can do about that."

Really? Well, Buffy, I have $1,300 down that says you should.

I went on two more dates through IJL before putting my membership on hold. I had ten more dates and ten more months left in my contract. But I didn't care.[7] It wasn't working out with IJL. I could see some thought put into matching me, though it seemed to be based on what I *don't* want, which is already how I choose men. After CPA Man, my counselors upgraded looks and creativity

---

[7] A month after my dates, I stumbled on www.consumeraffairs.com with complaints from former IJL clients. Their grievances ran the gamut: the company misrepresents their clientele, pay men and women who aren't clients to go out with real paying members so it looks like they have more clients than they do, are not capable of setting up decent matches, employ a revolving door of rude counselors, and refuse to refund money to dissatisfied clients. (Their contract is airtight.)

because those were the things I said were missing and I got Ren Man, who I said lived too far away, so the guy following him only lived three blocks from me. Unfortunately, he was also Angry Short Guy, so the fourth match was tall and cheerful. It seemed they had to fudge the looks category a smidgen for him, but I could have made another date with him work because we had chemistry. If only he hadn't been a born-again Christian and ultraconservative.[8]

I had a severe case of Goldilocks syndrome. Nobody fit and I was starting to think nobody ever would. I was going to be alone forever. I told this to Nan on our monthly lunch date at Chipotle and she sent me an email the following day with her thoughts.

> I think there is way more "not clicking" than "clicking" going on in life. I'm not sure you are "not clicking" any more than anybody else in this world, but maybe you feel like it's more noticeable because you're looking for it. I have no advice . . . just the observation that the only difference between you and others is you haven't met (or you don't recognize) your life partner yet. You will.

Yeah, but when? I started this whole thing thinking I'd simply see what happened while I checked out the dating process. But I threw in a silent contract for myself, which was that as soon as I started dating, I would meet someone I really liked and we would be together. This wasn't that far out of the realm of possibility, I

---

[8] Nothing wrong with any of this, but fundamentally speaking, it wouldn't work out, what with my socialist idealism and religious skepticism and all.

suppose. Most people want this when they date and lots of people achieve this. But these were heavy expectations for someone still learning the ropes. Unfortunately, I'm as impatient as they come, and when I've decided something, I want whatever it is to happen right then. And right then, I wanted a damn boyfriend and I wanted that boyfriend to be Justin Timberframe. Damn it.

Just because you can doesn't mean you should.

"You're doing an experiment about dating. How can you not go?" Edie, now two months pregnant, sinks into the guest chair in my office. Fatigue is kicking her ass. I feel the same way.

I got my first (and only) fan email after my article about the psychic readings ran, and Edie and I are debating the sender's viability.

> I read your articles with great interest and I too know how hard it is to date in this town. I'm a 40-year-old single guy who lives in Alexandria. I'd love to get together if you're interested.

"How *can* I go?" I coo to her belly because her peanut-sized zygote won't have a single thing to say that I don't want to hear.

I googled The Fan and found out he runs a Scrabble group. I also found a thumbnail picture. It was hard to tell *exactly* what he looked like, but I pieced together a professorial-looking man with round goggle glasses.

She throws my italicized argument back at me. "How can you *not* go?"

"I said I would only go out with people I am interested in. The experiment's supposed to mirror real life." I throw out the excuse, hoping she'll recognize this would be straying from my guidelines, even though I haven't followed them that stringently at all.

"What's the worst that could happen?"

I'm so tired of this mantra. What if? So what? Blah, blah, blah. It's so easy to say this when you get to go home and kiss familiar-smelling people hello every night.

"I don't know. What if he's an axe murderer? I can tell he's short."

My ridiculous concern is met with crossed arms and an unbudging smile. "How can you tell? It's a *thumbnail* picture. You don't even know that's him." Edie is so practical and convincing, even though I *know* he's short.

Up until now, maybe I've needed to go out with every single guy with a pulse who crossed my path in the interest of keeping an open mind and trying on all the sizes and styles before I commit. But I think I've reached the point where I *can* know when going on a date is a waste of my damn time. This is one of those times.

I was right about The Fan. He *was* short. I spot him among the bed heads bobbing behind laptops as soon as I blow in the front door of Tryst. He's sitting at a communal table packed with students pretending to study.

His eyeballs are magnified thousands of times behind Coke-bottle lenses, he's wearing white leather sneakers from the eighties, and has—no kidding—a smear of white zit cream dried on his forehead. He recognizes me from an online picture and waves as he gets up to greet me. With all of my heart, I want to leave—to run out into the snow and all the way home. The Fan goes in for a hug, which I thwart with a handshake. When we sit, the guy next to us glances sideways and half smiles through his short, stubby fingers, which are pressed to his mouth in prayer as he reads the paper. The man across the table with the salt-and-pepper beard is also looking on and contemplating. He's cute. I wonder how I can talk to him and give him my number without my date seeing.

I hate feeling this way, but I'm embarrassed to be with The Fan. But I try to stay upbeat and friendly and pretend that this is the most important thing I could be doing today. If I own the moment, maybe it will go smoothly.

Not exactly. It felt like one of the longest dates I've ever been on, even though I was in and out in fifty-seven minutes. No epic dates here. No sacrificing my time out of pity. That's no good for anyone. The Fan made it easy to speed up the process. He was a space invader of the worst kind. I can put up with some of the most obnoxious people on the planet, but the second they inch into my personal boundaries, I'm out.

The Fan didn't just lean in. He commandeered the back of my chair with his arm so I had to pitch forward into my cocoa to avoid what would have essentially been snuggling. He also grabbed my knee every time I said something remotely amusing, which was about every forty-five seconds, according to his laugh-o-meter.

And every five minutes I checked our neighbor's watch to see if enough time had passed for me to call it quits. I finally dragged out my premeditated lie about dinner with my parents and went home to do something more appealing like pulling out my eyelashes one by one and threading them back through with a rusty needle.

The one thing that did seem to be working out on some level: Justin Timberframe, who called me that night so he could hear my voice. That's what he said. I *could* imagine kissing him, and there's a part of me that thinks maybe . . . maybe this could be something. With talk of a potential meeting in New York, my head buzzes with hope.

"So what do you think it will be like when we see each other?"

"I think it will be great. Why, what do you think?"

He's not as positive about it as I am. "I dunno. It might be weird."

"Well, if you're going to ruin it . . ." I'm teasing, but also worried now that this is not a good idea, this meeting.

He laughs. "I'm not gonna ruin it."

Pause.

He's hesitant. "So."

Pause.

"Yes?"

"What do you think the chances are of us making out in the park?"

"Like, what do you want? A percentage?"

He laughs. "Yeah, I do."

"I'd say pretty good. A hundred percent. For sure."

"Really?"

"Yeah! Why wouldn't we? We'll be in New York. *At the same time*. It would be weird not to." I'm bold and swaggering. This is not me. But really, why wouldn't we make out?

"Okay." He's laughing at me. I think he thinks I'm cute.

Justin Timberframe emails me the next day. *You're just so damn cute.*

I knew it!

He sends me a book by one of my favorite authors for Valentine's Day. It's perfect.

PART II: EHARMONY.COM

"Ray-chullll." My friend Josh scolds me with his you-know-better voice when I confess that I'm going to sign up with eHarmony, which uses relationship science—an algorithm devised by scientists—to match singles. He and Kenneth have expressed their disappointment in my choice to pour cash into an organization that rejects gays. The eHarmony matchmaking system sifts through their applicants, plucking out and discarding 16 percent based on age (must be at least twenty-one), marital status (about 30 percent of applicants are already married so they get the boot, too), and inconsistent answers, which might indicate that you're depressed or can't be pleased, a category I could easily fall under. And they don't do gays, partially because their algorithms are designed to only match heterosexual singles and also because they're looking to match marrying types. Since gay marriage is illegal in most states, they won't match gay singles because the company says they "don't really want to participate in something that's illegal."[9]

I've thrown eHarmony into this part of the experiment instead of online dating because, while the service is indeed online, it's set up to select who you'll be put in front of based on a "revolutionary, scientific system" called the 29 Dimensions of Compatibility.

Apparently, the system screens each of the company's twenty million members to be sure he or she is "highly compatible with your unique personality," which sounds like it actually might be more effective than a human being with biases and a quota to meet. But I'm still skeptical, and I'm not the only one. While eHarmony has a significant research arm (called eHarmonyLabs, appropriately) and researchers with admirable credentials, there is still grumbling in the scientific community over the company's love algorithm and its ability to successfully match singles and produce happy, lasting marriages because there is still very little transparency with online matchmakers' research findings.

There are a few other things that have held me back from signing up in the past. Aside from the Christian underpinnings (the founding father of eHarmony is Christian clinical psychologist Neil Clark Warren, an affable-looking man with fluffy, white hair and the sedated smile of someone whose faith dissipates a single

[9] Almost three years after I completed this research, eHarmony launched a dating site for gay and lesbian singles called www.compatiblepartners.net in response to a potential anti-discrimination lawsuit.

cloud of cynicism within spitting distance of his halo), it's more expensive, almost double what I paid for Match.

A friend of mine has been on eHarmony for more than a year and has had decent luck. Nothing long-term, but she definitely gets past the first few dates and more into relationship territory. (This could very well have nothing to do with eHarmony and everything to do with the difference between our approaches to dating.) But every time she describes the process she goes through of putting people "on hold" when you're busy dating other people, and "closing matches" to say that you're not interested, it sounds like she's speaking Tagalog. I hope I get rejected.

I don't. I takes me thirty-two minutes to do the free personality test and my answers are funneled into a series of reports that describe my personality, and while I don't like admitting it, they nail me: Reserved, modest and private, doesn't like the spotlight, thoughtful, intensely emotional, reliable, bored easily, a little quirky, and needs a lot of quiet time to reflect.

The next step is to fill out a profile, and I answer questions about the three things I'm most thankful for, the person who's influenced me most, and the most important quality I look for in another person. It's *so* serious. IJL just wanted to know if I like street fairs and what color hair I prefer my dates to have.

Finally, I choose my "must haves" and "can't stands" from a prepared list that will eventually be sent to the men I choose to communicate with. "Must haves" include things like chemistry, autonomy, emotional health, and a sense of humor, and "can't stands" are lying, depression, materialism, worrying, and victim mentality.

I save my changes and, within two minutes, I get a canned email response from Neil Clark Warren: There's someone we'd like you to meet. Immediate gratification. So satisfying.

There are seven of these emails (one for each match). The first one, El Rico, looks promising. He's a smoldering Latino with a boyish smile, thirty-one, six feet tall, consultant, wants kids, and the most important thing he's looking for in a partner is *"someone who is able to face their world as it is, to determine how to improve it, and then act on that judgment. I like genuine people who have an affectionate disposition."* This could be me. But, like I always ignore the guy in the room I'm most attracted to, I don't email him. The stakes are too high. There's too much to lose. I'll wait to see what he does.

As for the other six matches, either the profile doesn't speak to me or their pictures say something else I don't like. Not to worry, the next day, the "matchmakers" at eHarmony have come through with seven more potentials, and three of them have requested communication. We've already lapped IJL in number of matches—and for $1,250 less.

I spend some time following the guided communication process with a few men while the matches keep coming. Guided communication is eHarmony's way of micromanaging the getting-to-know-you process. It starts with one person sending a set of questions to someone they're interested in. Then the match answers the questions and sends their own set of questions back. (If the match isn't interested or is busy dating he can put the person on hold or send an email saying he's not interested and give reasons why via a checklist eHarmony provides.) After another

Q&A exchange and must-have and can't-stand lists are sent, you go into open communication where you can email freely without the middleman. There is the option to go straight to open communication—called "fast tracking"—but eHarmony recommends sticking to their system.

I weed out matches based on location, profiles without pictures (of which there are many), and attractiveness. I know I should be more open-minded, but I've come to terms with the fact that looks are important to me, so I shouldn't be wasting any more time pretending otherwise.

If IJL had let me choose from their stack of potential matches, I wouldn't have gone out with a single guy. By rejecting handfuls of men based on their pictures, am I being practical and efficient? Or am I sabotaging myself? A little of both, perhaps.

After the first week, I'm still avoiding El Rico out of fear of rejection. I'm so tired of being afraid of the unknown. I click on the "start communicating" link and send El Rico my first set of questions.

The next day I get the email: Communication Received! El Rico responds to my questions with his own answers instead of choosing from the canned list of responses. I like this. My favorite was his response to my question "How trusting are you?"

I trust people until they prove me wrong. I also believe in second chances. I like this, too.

In my second set of questions, I throw in one of my own: If you were an animal what would you be and why?

His response: Rabbits do it better. Also they are the luckiest of all signs in the Chinese zodiac. It's my sign.

What do rabbits do better? Sex? My prude alert is on high. On the third day, he sends his personal email address with his last answer. He's turning his profile off because he's getting bombarded with matches. Me, too. Emails with matches jammed my inbox and I was having trouble keeping up. I put some on hold and closed others; some were requesting communication from me, but most were just smiling faces sitting there in eHarmony purgatory that I would never get to.

It means exactly what you think it means.

El Rico cuts through the top layer of bread and cheese on his onion soup and offers me a bite. We're both hung over for our brunch date. He's talking low and fast, and I can't tell if I make him nervous or if this is his regular delivery. He seems genuine, though, and when he reaches across the table to gently brush my bangs out of my eye, I melt. El Rico smiles softly and looks directly at me. I'm disarmed by his smoldering, earnest, cheesy heat.

"I used to live in this neighborhood, but I moved down the street. It's hard to live in an apartment again."

"Did you have a house once?" I set my fork down, giving up on my salad and turning half of my focus on El Rico and the other half on trying not to barf from the sticky layer of nausea that's formed over my internal organs from last night's alcohol binge that included playing flip cup until three a.m. at a party with people more than ten years younger than me.

He smiles sweetly and cocks his head to the side. "Yeah. When I was married. But we sold it."

A year ago even, I might have run the other way at the mention of divorce. But in his profile, his explanation was that he got married too young, they grew apart, and he's better for moving on. Very mature response. Maybe divorcés are the way to go. They know what they want and at least one woman has thought them worthy of commitment.

And why would I turn away a man who writes poetry? Haiku and free verse, he tells me.

"What about?" I quiz him to avoid talking because I don't feel capable of saying anything intelligent.

"Mostly about nature, some are erotic—wait—I mean romantic."

Did he mean erotic or romantic? Are those two ideas one in the same in his mind? He changes the subject. "I feel like I'm doing all the talking. Tell me about yourself."

Oh shit. On the spot. I root around for something interesting about myself. Marathon. I ran a marathon. Good choice. El Rico is a runner, too. Common ground. Easy subject to talk about. I can work with this.

"What *is* a runner's high anyway? I mean, I know what it is intellectually, but I don't think I've ever felt it."

El Rico's eyes are melted chocolate and he locks them on to mine. "Kind of like the feeling after a night of great sex."

My ears burn, but I nod knowingly and as clinically as I can. "Really . . . hmmm. Interesting."

"Yeah. It's like you're lightheaded, yet everything is really clear. Like after great sex."

Is El Rico trying to tell me something? Rabbits do it better, erotic poetry, great sex. However, it's been my experience that when someone is adamant about talking about great sex, it's just that. Talk. The reality is never as good as the chatter.

I nod again. Clinically.

I don't know if it's because my reaction is not enough or if he's so hung over, too, that he's experiencing short-term amnesia, but El Rico, once again, reiterates that a runner's high feels like the morning after great sex.

"That's what you said." I'm matter-of-fact. I won't give in to talking any more about great sex, or asking him what he thinks constitutes great sex. I haven't even showered, for Pete's sake.

He smiles at me again. What is it with him? I'm annoyed and drawn to him all at the same time. Even in my nauseated state, slumped over a slimy salad, my neck is buzzing and my skin is flushed.

El Rico hugs me good-bye outside on the snowy sidewalk. It's a meaningful hug that's surprisingly warm because he seemed so nervous throughout much of our date. He hangs on a little longer than necessary and sighs in my ear. "Mmmm."

The next morning at work he emails me a haiku about February sunshine and eHarmony bombards me with their daily seven. I can't possibly handle the volume of matches coming in. There's no rhyme or reason to most of the guys, some of whom live forty miles away. This match system seems to be playing a numbers game, and I'm doing the best I can to keep up. I'm now communicating with five men: El Rico, Music Man, David, Peter, and even one profile without a picture. He's Zenny: thirty-nine, six foot four, white, spiritual but not religious, doesn't drink or smoke. He's passionate about people who "strive for self and world awareness and live compassionately," and "admires all those who walk the path of love and kindness toward self and others." The sentiments are hokey, but I like it. We move through guided communication in three days, and in my last set of questions, I finally ask Zenny to put up a picture. I'm dying to know what he looks like.

He obliges. And this is where I end communication. I tried. I haven't grown as much as I thought I had.

This is also when I get a link to the eHarmony e-newsletter, which pops up in my inbox later that day.

WHAT "ALL OR NOTHING" SAYS ABOUT YOU.

. . . . All in all, though, it seems that chronic dissatisfaction and criticism of a mate may speak more to fears of disappointment than any real incompatibilities in a relationship. . . . Rather than seeing people as having both positives and negatives, overly critical people hold their romantic partners to an unrealistic expectation of having no faults whatsoever. Sadly, this type of "all-or-nothing" behavior can repeat over and over in one relationship after another until a person realizes that they themselves are the problem.

It's like the eHarmony folks knew I was casting people out for no other reason than I don't like their shoes. They're wagging their pious fingers at me, and while I find it condescending—because who are they to wag fingers at me; they're the homophobes—it still gets to me. I have a fleeting moment of clarity when I see that I'm terrified of getting involved with someone who disappoints me or leaves me empty and alone. I'm terrified of rejection, so I set my expectations so high that they can never be met, and I dig around with a magnifying glass looking for flaws in every person I date. There's *always* a flaw to exploit, and I'll find it so I never have to get too close.

The moment passes, I wipe the tears that flooded my eyes unexpectedly, and I return to a more subdued airbrushed bliss, clicking back to my matches page and ignoring the articles lying on my desk that need to be proofed. I tell myself I won't take a lunch break to make up for the time I spend scamming men at work. I double-check my progress with David and Music Man and decide to put Peter "on hold" even though I think the whole concept of "on hold" is obnoxious. I might as well write him an email saying I'm waiting for a better offer.

Aside from El Rico, Music Man is my favorite. He's six foot two, spiritual but not religious, plays guitar, and can do a cartwheel. We've been in guided communication for a week and a half and it's like riding through a forest on the back of an inchworm, though a welcome break from the warp speed of having a computer system churn out potential dates. He finally sent me his last string of answers to my questions and Dr. Warren's guidelines about how to act on a date pops up. I skip right over it to send Music Man an email.

There's a fine line between chemistry and leg humping.

"I want a slice of cherry pie." These are words you never want to hear when you're hovering somewhere between first and second base. It'd be like if Derek Jeter, instead of stealing second and making his way around the bases like he's supposed to in order to score a run, made a break for home plate by cutting across the pitcher's mound. You don't do it. But El Rico has the home-field advantage and he's making up the rules as he goes along.

He's kneeling above me on his too-firm Ikea couch; the kind with no arm rests so my head has been gradually inching off the end of it while we've been making out.

I reel from the cheesiness. "I can't believe you're using that line!"

"No, really, I didn't have dinner and I'm craving it."

I understand his pie fantasy to an extent, since I'd had my own on my first date with Music Man, who wore Vans, had a soft, strong nose, and a warm spirit. His energy was the opposite of El Rico's, who vacillated between nervous and uncertain to easy and romantic about every five breaths. The vibe surrounding Music Man was calm and steady and diffused the tension I'd been feeling before our date. We sat at an empty bar, smiling quietly and talking over the three-piece jazz band. When he told me he played guitar in the morning, that's when my pie fantasy began.

I imagined him in the kitchen I'd built for him in my head—it was painted lemony yellow with white trim. He's sitting in the breakfast nook at the oak table, his back to the windows thrown open to let in the early morning breeze and the faint perfume of the fuchsia peonies in the backyard. Sunlight slices a golden spotlight across his fingers as he glides through Bach. He's hunched over, but looks up at me to smile through the steam swirling from the mug of organic free-trade coffee on the table in front of him while I stand at the stove in my gauzy bathrobe and with bed head, eating spoonfuls of the half-eaten strawberry rhubarb pie I made for us the night before.

It was a sweet fantasy and there was nothing dirty or cherry pie about it.

I take partial responsibility for inviting El Rico's seduction scene into my life. I should have said no to his email inviting me to come over and listen to music and drink wine, which was an unequivocal sex invite, given all of his previous hinting around. That, and the bedroom kiss he laid on me after our second date. It took place in the middle of the street and in front of a young family with small children hurrying past us. I was starting to wonder if El Rico was using eHarmony for sex. It's typical of other online dating sites, but it would be surprising to find on eHarmony, since it's supposed to be more serious and marriage-minded.

To thwart any possible sex, I'd gone in prepared. This meant I actually *planned* for a night of sex, because everyone knows that shaved legs and lacy underwear guarantee no hookup. However, my theory is if I go in with full-coverage cotton underwear that comes in three-packs and with a five-day growth on my legs, it's altogether possible I could end up dancing around a pole.

So I shaved, put on lacy underwear, and even sprayed on some perfume. I was ready for seduction, and with the expectations set so high, there was no way they would be met. This I knew. Just to be sure though, I covered it all up with a benign uniform of jeans, Converse, and a hoodie.

That didn't work, and even though El Rico was adamant about *really* wanting a piece of cherry pie and not metaphorical pie, I was done. I was tired. I'd been fending him off for almost as long as I'd been there, which started off innocently enough with wine and music, as promised.

We sat Indian style on his couch, facing each other, delving into the more serious subject matter of third dates: families and religion. He worked slowly, easing in closer with each shift of topic, playing with my hair and caressing my shoulder and collarbone, not listening to a word I was saying. When he leaned in for a kiss, it took exactly one brush of our lips to turn his mojo on full blast. He was all over me, kissing, groping, gently pushing me back on the couch. I wasn't scared. I actually laughed out loud at the inanity of the situation as I lay there, palms face out in front of my chest in an upside down Cobra pose, head flung back for leverage as I pushed him off. "You gotta *slow down*."

But even at 50 percent, it all still smacked of a dog humping my leg. His hands were everywhere at the same time, peeling up my shirt, heading south.

This is where I enlisted the grabby-hand speed trap. "I don't think we're there yet."

"You're right; it's only our third meeting." He made it sound like a work conference.

After a five-minute wine break, he resumed his attack, squashing to a pulp any subtlety that might have been lingering with horrendous lines: "I have condoms;" "I think I'm going to take my pants off, it's hot in here;" "You have pretty eyes;" "I love your lips." And then cherry pie.

What happened to just making out—to taking your time and actually pausing to enjoy the moment instead of this mad rush to do it like teenagers bound by a curfew and car?

I sit up to indicate that we're done. He smiles at me with his cute half-smile. "I can take you home, or you can stay here."

I stay. It's too cold and too late to go home.

In bed, I curl up near him, but we're not exactly spooning because he keeps a pocket of air between us.

He turns on his side to look at me with his bedroom eyes. "*Que suenes con los angelitos. Buenas noches, chica.*" His voice is soft and, for the first time, he kisses me gently. I melt. But I don't sleep. El Rico snores, and I'm missing the three pillows I need to support my back that's out of alignment from all the arching I was doing to fend him off. By seven a.m., I've finally drifted into some semblance of sleep when El Rico turns to spoon me. This is when I realize El Rico is naked. He whispers in my hair, reminding me that he has condoms.

Oh, okay. It's the next day so technically it's our fourth meeting. The way dating has been going for me, we're practically common-law spouses.

The following night, I noticed the sky was my favorite color of indigo, which we'd talked about at some point, and I texted El Rico to tell him to look up. I was hoping to get out of the email-only zone and perhaps start talking on the phone. It seemed silly to be confined to written communication after sleeping with someone, except I was too afraid to call. The text message was meant to bring us one step closer. I'm not sure why I would use texting to take a relationship to the next step. Maybe due to the fear that he wasn't interested in anything more meaningful. Maybe because I wasn't sure if I was interested either. I'd rather play it safe than be rejected. Predictably, my text manipulation didn't work. He texted back. And rather dismissively.

I will check it out later. Enjoy it, chica!

A week and a half later I still haven't heard from Music Man. I'm disappointed, because I liked him, and I'm also relieved that I don't have to make a decision about him should I end up not liking him. It's a confusing combination of feelings toward someone I barely know. I console myself with the fact that if the cycle continues as it has over the past nine months, Music Man soon will be a distant memory like last season's dress that I had to have. And if there's one thing I'm 100 percent positive about, there's *always* another dress.

Almost two weeks later and exactly the day I decided to put Music Man out of my mind, I get an email from him. Guys seem to be completely obtuse when it comes to the nuances of nonverbal female communication, but they never fail to pick up on the screaming red light of disinterest.

Music Man wants to get together again, but he's traveling to Africa for two weeks. He'll email me when he's back. He doesn't.

He disappeared, until I jogged by him a couple of months later, and he was walking with a girl. They were definitely together. I pretended I didn't know him and wondered if he would even recognize me.

El Rico and I went out one more time and then he disappeared, too. I didn't like all the loose ends flapping around the men with whom I'd had no closure. I felt like my karma was becoming a whipping post. I thought eventually I would pay for my butchered breakups, though it never occurred to me that sometimes having things open-ended is okay, especially in one- and two-date situations.[10] So I attempted email closure with El Rico since it seems weird that we would sleep together but then not talk. The closure backfired because he wanted to apologize and make things right—and presumably keep dating. I didn't. I was moving on.

If we're talking numbers, eHarmony wins, hands down, with a whopping 357 matches sent to my inbox in one month. Over two and half months, IJL threw me into the ring with four guys. I can't even begin to do the math on the return on my investment for eHarmony because I'm terrible with numbers, but I know a deal when I see it, and 357 matches for $50 is way better than 4 for $1,300.

More important than quantity is quality, and the guys I met on eHarmony were much more my speed than IJL's roster, which

---

[10] Later, I learned that some guys prefer this type of arrangement because (1) they don't have to deal with uncomfortable feelings, and (2) it's an open-ender. They can always come back if they change their mind.

was exactly what I expected: buttoned-up and busy. (One date had to reschedule with me four times!) And really, what was I paying for? (I restarted my IJL membership after I completed the experiment and the dates they sent me on were even worse than the first time around.) It seemed like the databases over at eHarmony were getting more of a workout than Kiki & Co. But 357 matches were way too many to keep up with. eHarmony plays the numbers game. Not to mention that even though I turned off the "matching" function, so I'd stopped getting the daily seven and I'm no longer a paying member, the system continues to send my profile out to men as a potential match and I still get emails from guys requesting communication.

I don't deny the usefulness of either matchmaker, however. Even though IJL has been riddled in bad reviews, I can still see it being a helpful venue for people who need help finding dates and don't mind gambling away 1,300 bucks for only the small chance of meeting someone they will go out with again.

As for me, I've continued to come to terms with my own limitations, namely using superficiality as a defense mechanism; I judge so I don't have to get too close. But maybe it's not just me. Maybe part of the problem is the men in D.C. It's time to take my petri dish, which is now teeming with microbes, on the road and see what and who I'm missing out on in other cities.

Dating in Other Cities

A Lesson in Changing Scenery
(It really can do wonders.)

Supposedly, it's not where you are but who you're with. But you can't *not* take into account the factors that draw certain types of people to specific locales. People and cities are woven together to create a culture and a sense of place. Perhaps this could explain my general disinterest in the guys I'm dating. It's not fear of intimacy or that there are no good men. Maybe I'm living in a city where there are no good men *for me*.

People come to D.C. for politics and government, technology, and international affairs. And there are the lawyers. We have some creative types, too: artists, writers, designers, and musicians. But they are few and far between.

The one thing that does bridge the divide: no one is *from* D.C. You either have one foot in the door, ready to expend all of your energy on your career, or out the door and done with that portion of your life. Transient. That's what people call D.C., and it's my favorite excuse for why it's hard to date here. The word sounds so satisfying when you're using it in a particularly distressed way. "This place is so *trans*ient." The first syllable is long and nasal, and then it drops off, pinched and abrupt.

With all of this coming and going, local pride is hard to come by. You'd never hear someone from Chicago or New York utter a blasé, let alone negative, comment about their town. It's always pumping fists and pounding hearts. In D.C., it seems the pride of locals is wrapped up in hating the place, though happily, over the years, a certain satisfaction with the city has begun to emerge. I go back and forth on this sentiment. It's ingrained in me to want to escape because I grew up in the area, but if D.C. was really so abysmal, I would never have any fun and would have left long ago and stayed away. But I still wonder about my city's dating viability.

In its February 2007 issue, *National Geographic* crunched Census Bureau numbers and ran a map to compare the numbers of single men and women in major cities. The prevalent finding: West Coast cities have more men and East Coast cities are dominated by women. The numbers aren't that dramatic, though, especially when you take into account overall population.

Washington, D.C.: 40,000 more single women than men
New York City metro area: 185,000 more single women than men
Chicago: 40,000 more single women than men
L.A. metro area: 40,000 more single men than women
San Diego: 10,000 more single men than women
Charlotte: about 5,000 more single women than men

Aside from numbers, the map doesn't factor in essential data that would make it a go-to guide for singles. There's no breakdown of sexual orientation, ethnicity, overall attractiveness, and age, all of which would be deciding factors for anyone choosing to move to a city based solely on the number of single men or women.

And out of hundreds of thousands or even millions of people, would you really notice a crummy 40,000 difference in the number of men or women? I doubted it, but still wanted to test out the waters in other zip codes, just to see. I'll admit right now it was a botched experiment from the start, but this was my process:

I chose five cities/areas (New York, Charlotte, Chicago, Denver, Southern California) based on geographical diversity, population size, and the fact that I have some sort of a connection in each place to ease the process of getting a date. Some of the towns have made it to the "best places to live if you're single" lists. Some haven't. I think those rankings are suspect because D.C. was number three on one list, and if it were that great for singles, would I really be taking a fistful of my vacation time for this?

NEW YORK CITY

I had my year in New York back in 2000. I was twenty-seven. During those twelve months, I had four jobs, cashed two unemployment checks, got thirty-five mani/pedis, ran around the six-mile Central Park loop once, and went out with a handful of guys. It was the first time I'd ever dated around. I was just off a breakup with The Ex, and in the midst of a blurry breakup with a rebound. He didn't seem to want to let go, and I had no backbone to cut the cord. When I finally did, I started dating men I'd never in a million years be able to forge a relationship with; a collection of oddballs who hadn't left me with much more than a bunch of stories to tell.

This time, I have hand-selected the three people I will go out with: a friend of a friend, a man I found on the Onion named Dean, and Justin Timberframe. It's been exactly two months since I started plotting my reunion with him. So that's two months of wild and uncontrollable daydreaming about me in a frilly yellow sundress waiting under a tree, maybe by the boathouse in Central Park. He glides up to me, takes my head in his hands without a word, and kisses me.

There is no frilly yellow number because it's about two degrees when you take into account the flash-freezing effects of the winter wind; there's no Central Park because Justin Timberframe's train is late, and there is no immediate kiss because this isn't a movie. Instead, we meet at the corner of Forty-third and Sixth. I see him from across the street as we walk toward each other, him all teeth and smiles under his Red Sox cap. My heart backflipped and all of the what-ifs that had been crowding out my breathing capacity disappeared.

We embrace and kiss cheeks. Smiles are everywhere.

"Hi." I could eat him.

He smiles his toothy smile. "Hi."

"It's really nice to see you."

"Yeah. I thought I was going to be nervous, but I'm not."

"I know, me either." Liar. I'm a big fat liar.

We both keep smiling at each other. I search for words but there are none. A million nano-sized whirling dervishes have taken over every inch of my brain function, except the part that lets me feel happy and turns up the corners of my mouth.

"I saw a bar on the way over. We could go there." Finally. Words.

"I didn't think I'd be this excited to see you." Justin Timberframe looks at me across our table. I try to match his gaze, but I'm forced to turn away. It's too much. Everything feels incredibly intense. This is when I realize I'm leaning into the table, hands planted firmly on top, as if I'm about to pounce on him like I was on our date in D.C. "Like a moth to a flame." That's how Jeannine's astrology book (based on the week you're born, which is supposed to be way more accurate than the monthly variety) described my compatibility with Justin Timberframe.

I'm the moth, he's the flame, and the urgency to be near him makes me want to swipe the pints of beer in front of me onto the black-and-white tile floor, leap over the table, and tackle him. It's the most divine, most frustrating feeling ever because there's no practicality or logic to attach to it. This is tree-goring animal instinct.

Instead I hang on to the thread that is my composure and sit back, take a sip of beer, and pull myself back into the conversation, which is full of lulls. It wasn't like this before. Are these normal nervous silences or are we running into the roadblock of not having a single thing in common aside from the chemistry?

"Do you want kids?" Justin Timberframe is cutting to the chase. He's already made reference to what if this becomes Happily Ever After.

We're testing the waters and making sure we're on the same page for future plans. Why else bother continuing our long-distance tryst if, ultimately, something like not agreeing on having kids would tear the whole thing apart anyway? I'm not convinced this is the time or place to have this conversation, though.

"Yeah. If it makes sense." I lean my elbows on the table again, but I'm careful to keep my distance.

"So you might not want kids?" Uh-oh. We're entering into deal-breaker zone.

I scramble to qualify my statement. "I don't want to get married just to have a family. I think kids are a natural extension of a loving relationship."

"Well, I definitely want kids. I'm gonna make a great dad."

As our conversation evolves, I can't envision how anything will work out between us, but I push the thought aside.

Three hours later, in the middle of Times Square, Justin Timberframe and I say good-bye. I don't want to leave him. I feel like we're just getting started. I'm sad and impatient. I'm also drunk and don't care who has to push by our PDA bubble. We hug and kiss lightly and hug again. The mega-LUTS Day-Glo effect blinds me and I bury my face in the shoulder of his fleece in time to hide from the gravely voice hunched in the doorway of a pizza-by-the-slice joint that yells, "Get a room!"

* * *

Everything about Dean is black and streamlined—skinny jeans, skinnier scarf, and long, pointy boots. He's more handsome than his picture—angular face and hair that's still more pepper than salt. Instant attraction.

I wave from my chair, which is silly because, other than the guy on his laptop at the table by the window and the barista behind the old wooden bar, I'm the only one at our meeting place at a café on Mott Street.

"Hey." I stand up to shake his hand, which feels too formal, but I have no idea what to do. This might be the strangest date I've ever been on. I've been out with other guys who knew about the book, but there still seemed to be some authenticity to the affair. But now that I'm in another city, this actually feels like an experiment because the possibility of our relationship progressing beyond this date is slimmer than Dean's jeans.

He slides out of his jacket and hangs it on the chair back, leaving his scarf around his neck. He's gentle and deliberate with every motion, and has an aura of sincerity that's low and light, like the rumble of an alto clarinet.

Our conversation is sometimes awkward, but I'm stirred by this man, who makes his own furniture and invites me on his boat. "You should come out sometime . . ."

"That would be really fun . . ."

Every sentence seems to end on ellipses as we cope with the uncertainty of what this date is supposed to be. Even though I know exactly why we're on this date, I still have this overwhelming sense of, *What the heck are we doing?* And I get the feeling he does, too. Nonetheless, I imagine our day sailing, both of us in Docksiders with the heels beaten down and matching windbreakers—yellow, of course, because that's the recurring theme in my romantic-fantasy wardrobe—hugging and kissing as our hair frolics on the breeze.

I become distracted about halfway through our lentil soup snack, wondering if Justin Timberframe will be able to meet me in the park later to make out. I haven't heard from him since we hugged good-bye and we never set a time and place, so I excuse myself from my date with Dean to call him.

Once the much-anticipated makeout in the park is a go, all I can think about is getting back on the train uptown. It's ridiculous. I have this wonderful, handsome man in front of me, and I'm mentally tied up with someone else. I barely give Dean a chance because I've already mapped out my fantasy with Justin Timberframe—and while both of these relationships reside in the hypothetical because of geography, this pattern of becoming singularly focused on one person too soon and without reciprocity will play out over and over again.

The Central Park Makeout was a bust. It was one lousy thirty-second kiss. Justin Timberframe and I met at dusk and strolled for what seemed like an eternity and long enough for the temperature to drop and freeze the whirling dervishes. The chemistry waned with my patience. Neither of us made a move on our walk, unless you count when I looped my arm through his and leaned into him to make myself available, hoping to trigger something.

Insecurity took over. He could have changed his mind about making out with me. The mental gymnastics of wondering what he was thinking but being too afraid to ask were tiresome, so I decided to relieve the situation and steered us out of the park.

About five feet from where the path would dump us onto the sidewalk, Justin Timberframe finally woke up from his apparent sleepwalk. "Are we leaving the park? We haven't even made out yet!"

"We've been walking around for thirty minutes. I thought you didn't want to."

Frustration beat on my nerves but I turned toward him anyway and he kissed me. Finally. It was soft and gentle, but I was tense and chilled to the bone. A couple navigated around our spotlight cast down from the lamppost. It really should have been so romantic. But I felt like an imposter, which is how I always feel when I'm kissing someone in public (or on my stoop) who I'm not really *with*. I pulled back after thirty seconds. Our faces were inches apart and he smiled at me, grabbed my hand, and walked me back to the apartment where I was staying so I could get ready for my next date that was a silly, eight-hour drunken affair that ended on another ellipses.

I saw Justin Timberframe one more time before I left. Our brunch was stilted and quiet and either we had nothing more to talk about or we realized it was never going to work out, especially since we had no plans to see each other again. Ever. The hug and kiss good-bye was all sadness for me because when he walked away, the possibilities and hope that he represented walked off with him.

It took a couple months for our romance to expire slowly and quietly as the cancer of timing and distance filled the void. First the calls stopped, then the emails. And then, *phftt*. Nothing.

CHARLOTTE

Charlotte is not my kind of town. It's new and clean, and everywhere you go feels like the suburbs, even downtown. It's pretty, but there's no soul.

Even though Charlotte's nickname is "Char-lotta-guys," technically, there are more single women than men, according to the *National Geographic* map. The number of men did not concern me so much as the type of man I'd be working with. Based on my previous (and only) experience with Charlotte's singles scene, there was a preponderance of men in golf shirts wearing Bluetooth earpieces. I've also heard from several sources that Charlotte is a very married town. None of these things bode well for dating.

I set up a double-header for my visit. I have an afternoon date with Wine Boy, who I found on the Onion and dubbed Wine Boy because we're meeting at a wine bar, and dinner with my friend Anna's friend's cousin, who moved to Charlotte the week before.

I knew what to expect with Wine Boy. Blond, blue-eyed, banker, counts Pat Conroy as his favorite author. Cocky. Republican. Probably not very smart. I was wrong. Wine Boy was nothing like the person I typecast him as. He started doing yoga about the same time I did, and we talked all about his fruit fast and his upcoming trip to India because his bank job was no longer fulfilling. He was great, and if he lived in D.C., we would have happily gone out again.

I had no expectation for Anna's friend's cousin, except that she assured me that he'd be a good date.

"So, is he cute?" I grilled her for more details.

She teetered. "Weeeellll. He's balding and short. But he's *always* dating hot girls. I don't know what it is, but gorgeous women *love* him." This was supposed to give him street cred and, in a way, it did.

Apparently, he was a high-rolling model dater when he lived in New York—the very type I avoided like the plague when I was there.

"I really think you'll get along with him. He's sarcastic and outgoing—like you!" She also uses adjectives like *overwhelming*, *arrogant*, and *abrasive*, but this doesn't scare me off because Anna's threshold for these things is lower than mine.

Besides, confidence and a big personality go a long way with me.

"You look very pretty." Daddy Warbucks is staring at my chest when he says this to me across the dinner table.

"I can't believe you said that while staring at my rack." I'm laughing. I can't really blame him. I chose a dress with a neckline that zooms down well past regular low-cleavage zone. I let it slide because he owns up to his ogling and because he was the first guy since I started the experiment to bring me flowers. Anna was horrified because they were red roses in a plastic vase that he picked up from the gas station, but if she knew how low the bar had been set, she would have thought it was as wonderful as I did.

Physically, Daddy Warbucks is exactly as Anna described: short, balding, burly—but he also had the prettiest amber eyes. I towered over him in my three-inch wedges, which normally I'd never wear if I know my date isn't taller than me. But I figured if he dated models he'd be accustomed to it. He took us to Bailey's, a "hip" joint in Charlotte that has more of a dull drone than a vibrant buzz, and when the hostess walked us through the enormous open dining room to our table, I felt strong and secure with him behind me. He's capable. His confidence seemed to fill the room.

"So you were on a date right before this?" He looks directly at me.

I blush. "Sorry. I guess that's kinda weird." I feel like I've been cheating on him with Wine Boy.

"Ouch. I felt a little knife to the gut. I know we just met, but I'm a little jealous."

"If it makes you feel any better, this is probably the best date I've been on." And it was. We clicked right away. There wasn't that typical jig around the first-date elephant in the room because he called it out right away and squashed it.

"You know, you're the first girl who's been able to keep up with me. There aren't that many people quick enough." He picks up his lamb chop, sucks off the last sliver of meat, wipes his mouth with his napkin, and lets his hands fall on the table with a thump. The heavy links of his silver bracelet clink on the glass top as if to signal "Done!" I look down at my bowl of risotto, still more than half full. His race to the finish with his food makes me wonder what he'd be like to kiss. Hurried eater doesn't bode well.

Before the last bite of chocolate volcano cake, Daddy Warbucks is proposing to me, and seemingly only half kidding. I think about what it would be like to be married to this man. Secure, safe, fun, and, with the sparkle from two glasses of wine, I do feel some physical chemistry. I could kiss him.

We don't kiss though, because our date becomes a group outing with Daddy Warbuck's friend and my friends standing around a crappy bar full of men in polos with Bluetooths sticking out of their ears drinking Miller Lite. Just like I remember.

Even though there doesn't seem to be any competition (the ratio of men to women is about 2 to 1, so the ladies have their pick), the women are dressed to impress in halter tops, skirts that hug right below the ass, and cowboy boots.

I stray from my pack to find the bathroom and am accosted by a man in acid wash. I can tell by his mustache that he watches NASCAR. He pulls me aside and looks me in the eye. "Hi." He's brazen and doesn't think he needs to utter another word or do *anything at all* to keep my attention.

I put my hand on his arm and push him aside. "Excuse me." I can economize my words, too. I suppose I should have been flattered by his attention. Men in D.C. do not approach me like this. But it's fueled by arrogance. He's not interested in me. He just wants to know what he can get. Where are all the simple, down-to-earth men? I'm ready for a Midwestern straight shooter.

CHICAGO

"Sarah." We say it together, though there's no way The Psychic could have known my sister's name when he asked.

My date, a Chicago native (who is my coworker's brother-in-law's college friend) is a self-professed psychic. Actually, he calls himself "intuitive," and he proved it to me right then and there in Sushi Samba's lounge.

"You heard me start to say it, didn't you?"

The Psychic smiles at me, but he says nothing. He's six years younger, but he seems so much older right now.

"Seriously, how'd you know?"

"I had a feeling." He leans over to take a sip of his tea. The wax shifts in the candle he placed on the red leather banquette between us. I wasn't sure if this was an attempt to create romance or if maybe it was a premeditated move to create a scene where his powers would seem more legit. The wax shifts again as he sits back. The flame snuffs out.

The moment is over, which is fine by me. He'd been intuiting my existence for an hour, and before that, we chewed on our purpose in life, what it all means, and what happens when we die. I don't usually get into this subject matter anymore with anyone, date or no date. The stuff of religion, spirituality, and life is all very personal as far as I'm concerned, and not something to be debated or defended. And since I don't find many people who think about it like I do, I prefer to make it a non-issue. It was novel to have someone understand me, but all this scrutinizing only muddied the confusion over life I already feel. With every emotion dissected to death, I was crumpled up on the seat cushions, mentally wasted.

I'd been looking forward to meeting The Psychic and dating in Chicago in general. I love the city, and every time I visit, I'm overwhelmed by all the men. Friendly Midwestern stock.

The Psychic had dark curly hair, a happy grin, and he was tall. He was perfect. Still, our date had a rocky start. He looked scared across the table from me as we bobbled around introductory topics, and try as I might to ease the tension, he stayed behind an invisible boundary.

"So your book is on log homes then?" We'd been quizzing each other for forty-five minutes and not hitting on any similarities except that we both love unagi rolls, which led to a spirited discussion over the delicate sweetness of freshwater eel. We needed more.

I looked at him thoughtfully. I smiled. "No . . . it's on dating. That's why we're here. I'm researching dating in other cities . . ."

Relief washed over The Psychic and his invisible force field collapsed. He smiled a real smile and let his shoulders fall. "Ohhhh. I thought you were just horny. I've been trying to figure out this whole time how I was going to fend you off."

I'm mortified. I remembered the subject of my first email to The Psychic: *So my pimp, Troy, said I should contact you.* (Troy was our mutual friend.) I was only kidding, but I can't fathom what The Psychic was thinking. "Didn't you talk to Troy?"

He didn't.

"Wait. If you thought I was looking to hook up but you weren't interested, why did you agree to meet me?"

"Because I wanted to see what a girl who dates like a guy would be like."

Am I dating like a guy? Is this how they do it? And why didn't he *know* that I wasn't horny, that there's a bigger story behind our meeting? He's psychic, for Pete's sake.

He grins. He has the cutest dimples—and that accent. I wish I were ten hours closer and six years younger.

We're quiet on the cab ride home, and when he gets out at his apartment, there's no hugging or kissing. Just a long look good-bye. And the scramble for a second date. I was hopeful we could make it work, and we called each other a few times while I was in town to try to eke out another rendezvous. But he had his life and his job, and I had two other dates. They were back-to-back, the second date set up by the first guy I went out with, which made the first one less of a date because he wanted to talk about what I should do for my second date with his friend.

These were the kind of guys who love to talk about their town and their dogs—no frills, simple, easy, direct. I even set up my friend with one of them a few weeks later when she decided she wanted to start dating again. Of course, it didn't work out because he went for the boob grab in the car during the first kiss. Boys will be boys, regardless of zip code.

DENVER

With a nickname like Menver, how could I possibly *not* be able to find a date here? (The *Denver Post* even ran an article called "Odds

Stacked Against Men" because there are so many men compared to women.) And it's always ranking in the top three for best places to live if you're single. This should have been a no-brainer.

I still couldn't get a date.

I put out the feelers to my friends who live there, and friends of friends who live there. Not a single taker. One friend of a friend's excuse: "My friends are a bunch of pussies." That's not the rugged outdoorsy-man's-man persona I envisioned for Denver.

I went online to find guys, too. This time, I strayed from my usual routine and told the men I pitched to that I was going to be traveling a bit to Colorado for work. Log homes, mountains. It was a perfect ploy. I thought it was brilliant.

Pshaw. Brilliant nothing. Not a peep. I blamed it on the irritating fact that most of the profiles indicated they were looking to date in a much younger age bracket (eighteen to twenty-five) even though some of these men were pushing forty. But I already had my plane ticket and friends to see, so I visited over St. Patrick's Day weekend. It would be fun and I could certainly get a taste for the singles scene even if I wasn't actively dating.

My friend Carolyn attempted some last-minute setups. Her efforts yielded a ten-minute conversation with the bassist who was playing in the jam band we went to hear one night, and a body shot with the bartender at the après-ski bar. He was darling. I couldn't talk to him without blushing and having to pee. But the body shot—I wasn't too shy for that. I blame the Girl Scout Cookie shooters, which taste like Thin Mints, for the lapse in judgment. I'd never participated in an honest-to-goodness body shot, where you allow yourself to be mildly violated. I know the

PG version where you lick salt off someone's neck and shoot from a glass. And quite honestly, it's altogether possible I've never done one of those, either. But I was emboldened by Carolyn, who did one with her husband to show that it really is okay. So I hopped up on that bar as if I'd done it a million times and lay down with my belly exposed, careful to keep it sucked in so no one would be able to tell that I hadn't done a single stomach crunch in months.

With a whipped-cream happy face sprayed on my torso and a belly button full of amaretto, the bartender rubbed his hands together with glee and dove in. Literally, dove his face into my jiggly belly while I squealed behind a pair of beer-goggle glasses (the yellow lenses were shaped like beer mugs) that I insisted on wearing throughout the thirty-second fiasco, possibly in an attempt to hide that I'm way too old to be doing this crap.

Prior to the body shot, Carolyn and I were approached by the pasty moppy-haired guy from across the bar. He'd been trying to make eye contact with us for a while and I'd been averting my eyes and directing them on Carolyn's honking engagement ring so maybe he'd leave us alone. Alas, during the bar-wide St. Patrick's Day toast there was a fleeting moment when our pupils grazed. That was all Moppy needed.

"You girls wanna go back to my place to smoke some pot?" He came out of nowhere and launched his stealth attack, attempting to squeeze himself between our bar stools.

"You want us to go smoke pot with you?"

"Yeah. My condo is right over there. We could take some bong hits, get high. You know . . ."

"Bong hits. Then what?" I was dying to know what he was

going to say. Carolyn sat there in her green sparkle derby, smiling, watching, waiting.

"Whatever you ladies want!" He was so excited and sure of himself.

Our answer was a quick burst of laughter. There would be no bong-hit orgy or any variation thereof.

When I touched down on the tarmac two days later, my first voice mail is from one of the guys I'd emailed over the Onion whom I never heard back from. I'd sent my phone number out of desperation and he finally called. When I got home, there's an email from the other Onion guy. Maybe people in Colorado don't check email that often. Maybe they were off mountain biking or snowboarding or something. It was too bad. But I didn't care. I had my California trip in a couple weeks, and a much-anticipated date.

SOUTHERN CALIFORNIA

Your love life demands your attention—and not for the last time this week. You're likely to find yourself in over your head.

This was my horoscope the day I flew out to L.A. on the last leg of this month-and-a-half-long, multicity tour that had me exhausted and bleary-eyed. It couldn't have been more accurate.

I had one thing keeping me going: Superman. Beautiful, cocoa-skinned Superman, whom I found on the Onion last summer. I've never bothered with guys outside of my area code (except for this part of the experiment), but he was so . . . *so*. I had to make contact.

> Me: Will you move to D.C.? Please?
> Superman: Thanks for the love. If you're ever out in Cali, look
>   me up.

He included his personal email address.

I looked him up the minute I started planning this trip, and I emailed him again to see if he'd remember me and if he'd be into the idea of going on one of my bizarro dates. He was.

> Clear your schedule Saturday after 8 because you're all mine.

Will he take me to Chateau Marmont, where I will be sure to bump into A-listers in couture? This is definitely not a scenario for the brown cords and gray sweater I'd been schlepping around in all winter. Anxiety began to cripple me, because I had nothing to wear.

I called my friend Tracy, who I would be staying with. "What do people wear there?" She laughed at me. "Seriously. What should I wear on my date?"

"When I go out, I wear dark jeans, a three-quarter length top, and pointy shoes."

Same trend I've been consciously bucking in D.C. I always have to be different, and now I'm regretting it.

I called Patrick for a second opinion. He's in the industry, and when he gets dressed, it's like a costume change. Ripped denim and a black skullcap for going out in the city, stylized white button-down with a red embroidered dragon for a quiet dinner. He'd offer options.

"Skulls and crossbones are really big right now." Unfortunately, I ruled out that pattern last summer, deeming thirty-three too old for anything in the window of Urban Outfitters.

"What about for girls . . . ? What does Julie wear?" Julie is his girlfriend, who's a size two. It's pretty much useless for me to ask about her wardrobe because whatever it is will most certainly make me look like a whale and like I'm trying too hard.

"Well, when we went out last weekend, she wore low-slung jeans, a low-cut top, pointy boots, and a skinny scarf."

Exactly.

I had a vision of how I wanted to look. It included the lilac strappy top I saw at a boutique on 18th (that I didn't own), a pair of white jeans (which I also didn't own and didn't know where I'd find), and a pair of gold shoes (again, didn't own).

A Target shopping spree yielded nothing but mediocre gold wedges, so I deconstructed my existing wardrobe while Bart dove into a hidden corner of my walk-in closet and rustled bags that were probably housing a family of rats. For the long weekend, I ended up with three pairs of not-right jeans, one pair of linen chinos, a denim skirt, five tops, four tanks, one dress, five pairs of shoes, and the promise to myself that I can go shopping if I need to.

With wardrobe nailed down, I focused my energy on all the things I hated about my body and how, the minute I deplane at LAX, I will be cast out for being a size eight, plus five extra pounds. I went for a run with the hope that I could burn off the winter weight in one hour and if I stopped eating for five days.

"Put your finger in there." The Surfer points to a dime-size plant in the tide pool we're standing over. The Pacific crashes on Ocean Beach's craggy wall of rocks and sprays the backs of my legs. In my denim skirt and sandals that are definitely not meant for rock scrambling, I'm not prepared for this date. I was so preoccupied with my L.A. date, I didn't even consider what I would wear in San Diego. It's high noon and my winter-white shoulders are glaring in the sun. I'm vaguely aware that in a few hours my skin will be the equivalent of a boiled tomato, but the breeze over the Pacific suspends my denial. I wouldn't leave anyway. The novelty of investigating sea creatures on a date has plastered a smile on my face.

I stick my pointer in the tide pool, and the fan of leaves close around it with a gentle suck. I squeal and yank my finger away.

The Surfer laughs. "It's secreting poison. Won't hurt you, but bad for little fishes."

"What's it called?"

"Sea anemone or something." He smiles at me and shrugs his shoulders. Another sea spray sprinkles ocean over the front of his T-shirt. My, is he cute—like a blond-haired, blue-eyed version of James Mercer, the lead singer of the Shins.

The Surfer is also an artist and has that quiet calm I think a surfer must feel when he's floating out in the water, knowing he can just *be* as he waits for his wave.

"Are you sure it won't hurt me?" I'm being such a girl. But this date-by-the-ocean business with artists who surf and know a little marine biology is new to me.

"Probably not," he jokes, quietly examining another tide pool. He's determined to find me an octopus.

Eventually, The Surfer gave up on the octopus and we said good-bye.

"Thanks so much for our fun date." I smile shyly and shuffle back and forth. I go in for a hug. The Surfer goes in for a kiss. No ellipses here. It's an awkward composition of lip pecking and close-up smiles as he moves in and I pull away. It's strange to be kissing a stranger like this before three p.m. I wonder if this is just how dating is in SoCal. I give him one more kiss on the cheek and walk away, giggling to myself.

Biggie Biggie Biggie, can't you see, sometimes your words just hypno- tize me . . .

"Awwww shit. It's my *boy*." Superman starts dancing in his chair to The Notorious B.I.G. We're at a bar called the Hookah Lounge on Melrose and my gin and tonic is working with the morning's champagne as a pulley system, forcefully drawing my eyes to a close.

I had a long siesta after a three-hour brunch with The Adonis, who almost knocked Superman out of the running for Hottest Guy I Will Ever Date. But once the novelty of being out with physical perfection wore off, it was just a regular date, with a regular guy who was smart and successful, but with whom I had nothing in common. I seem to always stumble over the looks quotient in D.C., and now that I've been handed favorable aesthetics, I'm experiencing the realization that there needs to be a balance between form and function.

Superman and I had been traipsing all over Los Feliz eating frozen yogurt from Pinkberry, while I sunk further into my fatigue. I foiled our original plan to meet at a restaurant because I was late due to clothing drama (despite all of my preparation!). So he went to Plan B, which was a walking tour peppered with L.A. favorites, like the fro-yo and walking up Hillhurst Avenue to the observatory and pizza by the slice.

It was not how I envisioned our night. Of course, my vision had all sorts of pristine expectations attached to it, like we'd meet, fall in love, have babies with pretty cocoa skin, and live happily ever after with a view of the Pacific.

I look up at him bouncing in his chair, now to Jay-Z. Full lips, high cheekbones, warm brown eyes. I pick up a hint of his scent. Musky. Manly. He's exactly like his pictures. But the mystique started to crumble along our walk as he revealed that he is actually not immortal, but a twenty-eight-year-old guy who loves comic strips and cooking, wants to write screenplays, and counts Biggie Smalls as one of his role models because he used to be the same size. He used to be the fat guy—three hundred pounds fat.

I'd been worried that I wasn't going to be perfect enough, pretty enough, and skinny enough for this date. And of all the people who would understand . . . the irony. I think of the hours wasted twisting around to inspect my ass in the mirror and now want to kick myself in that ass.

We dodge past the bumping and grinding on the dance floor and find a spot under a heat lamp on the patio. We turn to each other, and when he starts to move, I forget how to dance. How can this be? I love to dance. Dancing is my *thing*. I'd much rather dance than talk at a bar. I take dance classes. I can dance. But not now. I shift my weight from one foot to the next, trying to follow some semblance of a beat, but I'm all rigor mortis.

I don't know where to look or what to say or how to move. Superman is inching in, trying to close the invisible barrier between us. He holds the small of my back and pulls me to him.

Our bodies are barely touching and I'm vaguely aware that my strapless bra is sliding down around my stomach. But I'm too distracted by his presence, which creates a bubble of safety and warmth from the gravity-defying threesome behind us—a boisterous redhead with boobs tumbling out of her white tube top as she bends over, grinding her enormous butt into the skinny ass of a guy who's grinding his crotch into another girl with gold hoops and hot pink pedal pushers, which, as I note when she turns around, accentuate *everything*.

I bury my face in Superman's neck and he lets his cheek drop down to mine. He kisses me. And there I am, making out on the dance floor of an L.A. club while the DJ makes his fourth shout-out to a Clipper's player nobody cares about and the threesome flips their sandwich.

"I want you to come in." Superman is peppering my face with kisses, trying to coerce me into his place when I drop him off. "We don't have to . . . *you know*." We'd been making out in my rental car for about forty minutes. His first pitch to get me inside was to play with his roommate's new puppy. The let's-go-pet-the-animal line isn't a bad line, but it's so transparent. Men (and women) should just say, "Let's go inside and make out. I will probably want to have sex, but we don't have to." Kind of like what Superman is saying to me now.

If I go inside with him, there's no way we're not going to . . . *you know*. And while it's very tempting to throw caution to the wind and go in and . . . *you know*, I don't. If there's one thing I've learned during the last few months, it's that sometimes, things are better left unsaid. I want to preserve this perfection. I kiss Superman one last time, push him out of the car, flip on the defroster, and drive off, peering through the bottom of the windshield that's starting to clear.

I'm beginning to understand men and their motives (boobs and sex), and the fact that, when you drill down to the basics, they're very much the same no matter where you go, for better or worse. Confident, shy, bold, uncertain, nervous, curious, nice smelling. I felt a special affinity for the men I went out with while I was traveling because they all agreed to be part of my experiment without knowing much or anything about it. They just wanted to go on a date and they weren't afraid of this big old unknown, which was just little old me. I learned a lot from this approach about being open-minded and that sometimes it's fun to go along for the ride even if it doesn't dump you off at the end of an aisle in a pretty white dress. But I can't honestly draw real conclusions about what men are *really* like in other locales since I went out with so few. And, of course, there was always that one inconsistent variable screwing everything up—me. But I'll make sweeping generalizations anyway, just for fun.

If we're talking pure aesthetics, California ranks highest, which is not news. Pretty faces and toned bodies are everything there. If we're talking down-to-earth, solid straightforward men, Chicago is the place. Artsy and a little out-there with great style? New York. Don't care about having to weed through morons and trillions of married couples for a boyfriend who most likely works in finance and could fully support you? Move to Charlotte. Love body shots and bong hits? Head West to Denver.

I remember thinking during each date how I wished I could import each guy. "If he lived in D.C., I would go out with him again." I said it after every date. More telling, as I went along, I kept thinking each date was the best date ever. It wasn't because the guy I happened to be out with was better. It was because I was finally letting myself have fun. I knew I would never have to commit to any of these people or deal with a "breakup," so not only did I go out with men I would never consider dating in D.C., I realized that I *could* be attracted to someone who was short and balding as much as I could be attracted to someone tall with a full head of hair.

And because I stopped attaching expectations—I didn't have a single vested interest except getting the date and going on the date—I was more relaxed, the atmosphere was more relaxed, and my date probably got a better feel for who I am. It *was* better. If only I could rewire my brain to actually do this when I'm back home.

This change in perspective was reinvigorating, but I don't believe moving to a new town to overhaul your dating agenda makes a lick of sense. Changing geography doesn't change anything, because you are still the same person with the same problems and same neuroses.

This is where the dating self-help books come in. They'll require me to look inward to clarify what it is I'm looking for in a man. There has to be some bit of advice, a droplet of wisdom, a mantra to repeat over and over, that will get it through my head that a date is just a date.

Dating Books

A Lesson in Ditching the Ideal

Fragile pink bunches are bursting all over town. Cherry blossoms. It's officially spring in D.C. The air has gone from a bone-chilling, clammy thud to a delicate tiptoe almost overnight. The scent is sweet and expectant, and it always evokes those random memories of things and people you hadn't thought of in ages. This spring, it's Jonah and a morning the year before when he and I got up before work to walk around the Tidal Basin under the peaking cherry blossoms. We held hands and hugged, and one of the hundreds of photographers documenting the bloomfest snapped our picture while I leaned back into him and he propped his chin on my head. It was perfect. At least the memory is.

I met Jonah on the Onion when I first started researching the article I wrote on dating self-help books. Our first date tested out how I would actually go about implementing dating-book advice in real life. I used *The Rules: Time-tested Secrets for Capturing the Heart of Mr. Right* by Ellen Fein and Sherrie Schneider.[11] Before I met Jonah in person, I had an inkling of interest in him about the size of the mole on my back. But I actually ended up liking him. He was smart, tall, and wore red Pumas, and he liked to make me laugh. It was the first relationship I'd had in three years that outlived the soy milk in my refrigerator.

I hadn't heard a peep from Jonah since I sat across from him on my couch while we both pretended to be sad over our breakup. We vanished from each other's lives without a trace, making me wonder if I actually imagined the whole thing.

Exactly one day after this musing, Jonah emailed me and wanted to catch up.

And so we did. Over dinner at the Reef, I waited for Jonah to tell me why we were *really* there, because it didn't feel like a catch-up. It felt like he was sussing things out—investigating possibilities and opportunity cost. Then, he told me about the woman he almost dated a couple months before. He pursued her when he thought he had no chance ("There's something sexy about a woman who's not interested."), and when she was finally receptive, he dropped the whole thing under the guise that he was too busy.

---

[11] It's the retro advice a grandmother or prissy great-aunt would spell out over tea and crumpets: "The purpose of The Rules is to make Mr. Right obsessed with having you as his by making yourself seem unattainable."

Sounds exactly like when I dated him. I played hard to get with *The Rules* on our first date and he couldn't wait to go out again. But as I eased into the relationship, he started concocting a schedule that boxed me out.

"What did he want?" I'm in Mike's office, lying on his couch the morning after the meeting. I'm flustered and confused by the drama that the interlude drummed up.

Mike swivels his chair around and begins his lecture. "It's springtime. Nature is spreading its seed. He's coming out of his winter nap, scratching his balls, and wondering, who can I implant? He's got nothing on the horizon so he starts thinking about who he already knows. He thinks 'Rachel! She's cool and smart and pretty. We had fun! I think I'll give Rachel a call and see what she's up to, maybe she's in the mood for a little cross-pollination!' You can't blame a guy for trying." He sits back in his chair and crosses his ankle over his knee, cackling.

That's it? Is it really as basic as "my loins told me to say this/do this/act this way, so I did?" Are men really that primal and visceral? I think the answer here is yes, and while I will never understand it, maybe I'll learn to accept and even love it.

I don't follow up with an email and neither does Jonah. What's the point? We're not going to be friends. And my golden rule is never, ever redate someone. You broke up for a reason, and nothing good ever comes out of Part Two. The second time around leads to more heartache and wasted weeks, months, and years, and is directly related to not being ready to move on. It's settling. Experience has solidified this for me.

Playing hard to get always works—at least initially.

"Well, it was nice to meet you." My date hops up from his stool and offers his hand to shake, pretending to be on his way. Handshake Guy is a twenty-five-year-old law student I met on eHarmony who gave equal weight to social justice and the Yankees on his profile and showed up for our date in a suit and tie and carrying a backpack. We'd been drinking beers at the Diner, where indie people with funky hair serve pies and meatloaf. "Bootylicious" is blaring through the speakers and I'm trying out *The Rules* (again). I'd gone to Barnes & Noble in the suburbs, plopped down at a long wooden table with a stack of dating-advice books, and rifled through selections until I found a diverse sample of titles. The others I would be testing out, in addition to *The Rules*, were: *The Surrendered Single: A Practical Guide to Attracting and Marrying the Man Who's Right for You*; *Be Your Own Dating Service: A Step-By-Step Guide to Finding and Maintaining Healthy Relationships*; and *Turn Your Cablight On: Get Your Dream Man in 6 Months or Less*.

I picked the Diner specifically because it's in my neighborhood. (*Rule 4: Don't meet him halfway or go Dutch on a date.*) But he was making it very hard to be "a creature unlike any other"[12] though,

[12] According to the authors, this is "the way you smile (you light up a room), pause in between sentences (don't babble on and on out of nervousness), listen (attentively), look (demurely, never stare), breathe (slowly), stand (straight), and walk (briskly with your shoulders back)."

with his verbal ribbing, which elicited a cycle of snappy comebacks from me about his backpack and tie (*"Rules Girls" are not sarcastic*), which in turn fed his mock handshake-and-leave routine.

I mentally review *Rule 9: How to act on dates 1, 2, and 3*. Specifically, don't daydream about the future or fantasize before the date; don't be serious, controlling, or wifey; don't mention the *M* word (marriage) or feel obligated to fill up conversational lulls; let him do all the work in picking out the restaurant; laugh and smile. The goal is "nothing and being" and to not try too hard. I'm already struggling with that advice.

I swat at Handshake Guy's outstretched hand.

"You know I'm kidding, right?" His voice is low and booming. He's the whitest-sounding black guy I've ever heard. Whiter than Eddie Murphy imitating white people. He also listens to jam bands and Southern rock, the whitest of white music.

He sits down and I wait for him to launch into a new topic. *Let him do all the work.* I smile at him. He smiles back and sips his beer. He has the prettiest teeth. They're the perfect size, shape, and color. I want to tell him so, but I'm not sure how compliments play into *The Rules*. So I wait. Nothing. We sip beers and look at each other out of the corners of our eyes.

"So, do you have to wear a suit every day?" I spit out the question before I even realize I'm breaking *The Rules*. There was too much silence. I implement the book's recommended hair comb[13] to recover my femininity.

---

[13] Tilt head and comb hair back from the forehead with fingers in a slow, sweeping motion.

"No, no, I was in court today." He loses me after three minutes of talking about his case. I paste on my sugar-free smile because I can't think of anything lighter and airier than that, rest my elbow on the bar, drop my chin in my hand, let my toe land on the footrest of Handshake Guy's stool, and launch into the ticking off of my mental pros and cons list. Cons: He's slouchy, definitely *not* five foot nine, like his profile said, and his nails are bitten to the quick. Pros: He's confident—and those teeth.

". . . and I have a job lined up in New York for September . . ." My ears burn. He's leaving. Why am I out with someone who's leaving in five months' time?

"Another?" Handshake Guy is pointing at my dwindling beer.

The Rules said I have two hours for a drink date. But I'm actually having fun. I'd been bellyaching all day about not wanting to go out with Handshake Guy because I'm missing out on a night with my friends. It was an important night, too, because Jeannine was making her debut with her ex-boyfriend, who, like Jonah, had found his way out of the woodwork, having decided he wanted to be with Jeannine. Nine months ago she could barely get him to call once a week, and now Ben's showing up at her door with flowers, demanding her attention, professing his love, and generally not taking no for an answer. I was skeptical because of my golden rule about redating, but maybe people can change, and if they can, Ben is setting the example.

Handshake Guy informs me that he was captain of the track team in high school and holds the record for the high jump. It feels foreign to talk about high school achievements because that was fifteen years ago for me. But that's what he's working with.

"So how high can you jump?"

"Well, back then, it was six feet, but I couldn't do that anymore."

"Could you jump on this bar top?" I grab the metal edge of the counter, which is about four feet high.

He sizes it up. "Sure."

"You could do that from a stand?"

"No way! I'd probably have to take a step."

A step. I begin to feel tinges of what seems to be attraction. Maybe it's the second pint, maybe it's the fact that I discovered we are both very serious about French fries, but being able to jump six feet high might actually be sexier than being six feet tall.

Rule #11: End the date first. After two more handshake incidents, I call an end to the date. Handshake Guy made it easy to follow the rule about not going Dutch. He palmed the bill as soon as it hit the counter.

"I feel like I should walk you home." We're standing on the corner of 18th and Columbia by the McDonald's. "Everybody Wants to Rule the World" is blaring from the loudspeakers above us.

"That's crazy. There are tons of people out. Not necessary." Also, I wanted to make sure I didn't have to deal with *Rule 14: Keep kissing casual on first date and don't invite him up to your apartment*, which goes with *Rule 15: Don't rush into sex.*

"Well then . . ." Handshake Guy slings his backpack over his left shoulder and holds out his right hand.

I ignore it and hug him. "Thanks for the beers. It was fun."

"Yeah! We should get together again! I mean, if you want. I wouldn't hate that."

I wouldn't, either.

Aside from Handshake Guy, my dating well is dry, so I put the feelers out for more men. I'm on eHarmony and the Onion, I email friends for setups, and I'm shooting smiles at every male stranger standing close enough to see the whites of his eyeballs. I've become shameless in hunting down more dates so I can test out the next book, *The Surrendered Single* by Laura Doyle,[14] whose approach is to surrender to the desire to be happily married. For some reason, this makes my throat tighten. I want to get married, but it scares me because what if I choose wrong? "A surrendered single doesn't have to look for Mr. Right—she attracts him." You let the man take the lead and the only thing you control is yourself, thoughtfully examining your feelings throughout the dating process. You graciously take compliments, focus on your own happiness, show vulnerability, end dead-end relationships, and, my sticking point, ditch the idea of the perfect guy. A checklist is a "suit of armor," according to Doyle, and it's time for a costume change. No more height, age, education, and income requirements. My new outfit is a flexible spandex jumpsuit in which I can truly let go and let flow.

There's a quiz: "Are you attracting the man who's right for you?" I score 70 out of 100. I'm willing to risk my heart and there's nothing to stop me from having a passionate, intimate romance—except for all my baggage.

In therapy that week, I dissect the baggage problem. I'm

---

[14] Doyle's credentials: author of *The Surrendered Wife*, holds lectures and workshops, and is founder of online singles' meeting place surrenderedsingle.com.

worried that I'll never have a fulfilling relationship because I'm still working through old issues of not feeling like I deserve the attention and affection that I need, and so I recycle a pattern of being attracted to men who can't give this to me.

I look directly at Judith, which I never do because eye contact is always fleeting in our group. "Seriously, am I doomed to fail? Because I don't know if I'll ever be done with working through this stuff." In her tricky way, she gets away without answering, which brings me to the conclusion that I'm missing the point. I wish I had her bird's-eye view. My life would be so much easier.

In the meantime, I throw myself back into the mosh pit with a couple new prospects online. There's Yogadancer on eHarmony and Pauly on the Onion. I am not the least bit interested in either of them. I've seen Yogadancer on other dating sites but always pass him over because there's something about his smirk that is unsettling. And he's short: five-foot-seven short, which could mean five foot five. However, I see in his profile that he's into a holistic lifestyle—yoga, massage therapy—and was a dancer. I'm into these things, so there's lots of common ground.

As for Pauly, I would normally never consider going out with him because he looks tubby in his pictures and there's nothing I connect with in his profile. But in the spirit of Doyle's instructions to "accept all the offers that come to you unless he's the creature from the Black Lagoon," I surrender and answer Yogadancer's questions and email Pauly back. Maybe this is when I meet The One, when I toss out all my rules.

I crack open another book, *Be Your Own Dating Service* by therapist Nina Atwood, for ideas on how to find more dates.

Chapter 4, "Looking for Love," is all about the search. However, it's not about the search for men online or through friends, but the search within yourself to define what you're looking for. I need to create a vision statement and make some lists of my criteria.

This completely contradicts *The Surrendered Single*, because I thought I was done with lists, and in retrospect, maybe I should have picked one book and stuck with it, because this is a lot of information to consume all at once.

However, Atwood's lists are about nonnegotiables, which do not include superficial items like hair color and height. There's a list for these, too—the negotiable list. Nonnegotiables are bigger-picture (and often obvious) things like "no drug addicts." But it's essential to establish the points that we might take for granted.

For the vision statement, the idea is to focus on the kind of relationship I want to have rather than personal characteristics of a man. I scribble my statement and criteria on three yellow stickies:

VISION STATEMENT

Open, expressive, harmonious. We laugh a lot and do nice, spontaneous things for each other. Reciprocity. We take care of each other's needs while offering the necessary personal space. We like to do fun things outside of the house together. We hug, hold hands, and kiss. We aren't defensive. Respect is essential, as is love and a strong physical connection. My partner is not bound to tradition, is firm in his beliefs but understands that his way isn't the only way.

NONNEGOTIABLES:

Not addicted to anything
Loves to laugh
Deals well with stress
Handles problems immediately
Makes a comfortable home for himself
Doesn't smoke
Eats well and exercises
Respects my choices and is not belittling
Knows life is as important as work
Open to new perspectives
Always willing to try new things

Atwood's dating curriculum involves knowing how to spot an "available" partner. She uses a train analogy. I'm looking for (and to be) a Northbound Train, which is someone who has healed from and takes responsibility for failures in past relationships, who looks within for self-esteem rather than relying on someone else, who exhibits responsibility and integrity, is self-supporting and self-nurturing, is in touch with his thoughts, and can express feelings and needs, has no addictions, and wants to be in a relationship—with me. Easy enough.

There are three other trains to avoid at all costs: Southbound Trains, who aren't available for a relationship and have no desire for one with you (e.g., Dave Grohl and other musicians and movie stars); Eastbound Trains, who *are* available for a relationship but have no desire for one with you (Rafe and other single people who don't know you exist); and the mother of them all, the Westbound Train, which will let you on board only to dump you off with a hole in your heart. This person will pursue, ask for dates, fall in love, be monogamous—but he'll (she'll) always hold back and never commit. "Just when you think you've finally found 'the one,' the Westbound Train will slip through your fingers, leaving you hurt and confused." Signs of a Westbound Train: Starts out hot and heavy then fades suddenly, cancels dates at the last minute or waits until the last minute to ask for a date, is late or doesn't show up, never invites you to his home, is defensive about past relationship, blames the ex or is still loyal to her, doesn't court you, voices fear of commitment or reluctance for monogamy, avoids the "you and me" discussion, and lets you do all the work.

This is a lot of information to process. I've entered into a new realm where getting the dates is a cinch and not the obstacle I must overcome anymore. The task I'm saddled with now is pulling apart all this advice, understanding myself and what I truly want, and forming a structure I can follow while I'm on the date.

Some frogs kiss really, really well and are worth kissing.

I meet Handshake Guy at the Russia House in Dupont Circle, where I break all second-date rules. We drink lots of vodka in the dim lounge that pulsates velvet red all around us. We also thumb wrestle, and he shakes my hand and threatens to leave at least five times.

"You're Handshake Guy. That's who you are!" I'm drunk from gimlets and no food and have no problem revealing the alias I've made up for him. He laughs and replaces the handshaking with high fives. We stay out for hours, which, according to *The Rules*, I'm not supposed to do on the second date.

Handshake Guy once again refuses to let me pay, and he walks me all the way home, holding my hand, even though he lives two blocks from the bar and I'm about a mile away. Northbound all the way . . . *except* for the part about him not being around here much longer. I don't remember anything about people leaving town. Should I even be incorporating other book advice into my relationship with Handshake Guy when I started off using *The Rules* with him? It's hard to ignore what I've already learned. Deal with it later. Too many gimlets to care.

At my stoop, me midbabble (yet another rule I'm breaking, though I can't remember which one), Handshake Guy kisses me. And, oh my, he does it very well. Handshake Guy wins Best Kisser of the Year. Maybe of the decade. Maybe ever. If I hadn't been standing on my stoop kissing *yet another guy*, I could have kissed him for hours. But it feels like the windows across the street are balcony seats to the dramedy that's been unfolding on my stoop over the last nine months. That, and the chemistry—I'm not sure if it's there. Clearly there's something, but I don't know if this is the real thing or the faux-drunk variety. I go with what I do know, and I know he's a good kisser. And I grab one more before hugging him good-bye.

Not only does Handshake Guy get tens across the board for kissing, he gets a perfect score for etiquette when he calls the next afternoon to say he had a good time and wants to make sure he can see me again. He said these words. It's unprecedented. He pays, insists on walking me home, is a dreamy kisser, calls right away. Maybe Handshake Guy is following his own rules. He might be eight years younger, but he has most of the men I've dated beat when it comes to dating protocol. Is it *The Rules* working? Jonah made the same follow-up call after our first date. Of course, this is technically my second date with Handshake Guy, but even so, of the dates I've been on for this experiment, few, if any, have made any follow-up *phone call*, ever. Email or text message, yes. But the phone call is huge.

Intrigued . . .

I've seen this subject line a zillion times before from guys I meet online. It's completely overused, but I can't help but love when someone is intrigued by me. The email is from Jeb. He's thirty-eight, and in the world of online profiles, is perfect. There's something about the way he weaves the tale of himself and what he's looking for that beckons to me and makes me want to jump around, shouting, "That's me! That's me!"

Three email volleys and four days later, I give Jeb my work email address, finish up guided communication with Yogadancer on eHarmony, and have a new prospect with one of my chiropractor's friends. And then there's Pauly, with whom I've exchanged intermittent emails but keep forgetting about because I'm not interested. At all.

I read in one of the dating books that even if you meet someone you like, you should keep dating around. What I really want to do is meet Jeb, fall in love, and live happily ever after. He gets dreamier with every email and I have issued the blanket statement that if there's no chemistry when we meet, "I will cry." I get Jeannine's official seal of approval during one of our Thursday dinners when I let her read every last email Jeb and I have written to each other. "I think *I* like him!" She grabs my arm and shakes it excitedly. "He's special."

Jeb finally asks for my number. We do a dance of phone tag and a brief "I can't talk now" conversation while I'm out to dinner with Ethan, who's moving. Ethan and I hadn't talked much since January because he'd been traveling for work and I'd been busy dating. And now he's leaving and I feel abandoned even though our relationship isn't a constant source of attention for either of us. I'm sad that we're veering away from each other again. I've heard that when someone leaves your life, no matter who it is and what that person means to you, it's supposed to be a good thing because it automatically frees up some of your emotional and mental capacity. Maybe you didn't ask for it, didn't want it, but nonetheless, it's one less person to concern yourself with. Maybe Ethan's leaving frees me a little. He can no longer be a Plan B, C, or D, which, no matter how clear I am on our ambiguity, is always there. There will be no more wondering about the "if" with him.

Besides, there's Jeb—Jeb and his scratchy voice that infects me with goose bumps. I can't stop thinking or talking about him. With everyone. With that silly look on my face.

Even though I haven't met him, he makes wanting to date other men really hard.

Yogadancer is standing outside the vintage clothing shop in the Maryland suburbs where we're meeting. According to *The Rules*, I should have made him come to me, and I wish I had because getting up to Takoma Park by Metro on a Sunday is a ridiculous pain in the ass. It took forty minutes to go seven miles. But I'm surrendering today. His back is to me, but I know it's him. I'm not sure what I thought five foot seven would look like, but it definitely wasn't this short.

"Hi." I peer around his right shoulder and he turns and smiles back at me. I don't flinch even though he's not what I was expecting, because there's no list to check off. According to *The Surrendered Single*, I am the "Goddess of Light and Fun, who's quick to laugh and never stodgy."

I reviewed first-date instructions before I left my apartment. The idea is to be quiet (this allows women to be more "observant, confident, feminine, and receptive"), not to control the conversation, and set the stage for a relationship by letting my date know what I expect. I'm to listen to him and my own feelings about how I feel when I'm with him.

I surrender and prepare myself to receive.

"Hi, great to meet you." He goes in for a hug.

I pull back. He smiles at me. I wait for him to make the move.

I'm not controlling or manipulating. "Want to go over to the market?"

"Sure!" I'm light. I'm fun. I'm a goddess. I actually don't feel this way at all. I don't know that I ever have. But I will try.

I'd envisioned a date where we'd walk from the lettuce stand to the bread stand and talk, drink coffee, and then I'd be on my way. Light and easy. This market though is exactly one block long, and in five minutes, we make our way past the tables of bright, fresh produce managed by market people with long hippie hair and nose rings. I'm trying to ignore the backpack slung over Yogadancer's shoulder that, for some reason, bothers me as much as the white leather tennies and sunglasses hanging from Croakies. I acknowledge these misdemeanor crimes of fashion and I move on. Just like in yoga during shavasana. Acknowledge the thought and clear the mind.

We stop and look at each other. I pause, waiting, looking into his droopy dog eyes. Surrendering. Sort of.

"You're much more beautiful than your pictures. Usually people don't look as good as their pictures."

I blush and break the no-modesty rule. "I don't photograph very well." This is not receiving graciously, which is the key to surrendering and the essence of feminine behavior. "Rejecting the gift is rejecting the giver." I don't want to reject gifts or givers. I will receive from here on out.

Yogadancer goes on like I didn't stomp all over his gift. "Well, it seems like this is the end of the market. It's smaller today. Did you eat?" He's eager to turn this into a real date.

I'm not hungry at all, but I'm agreeable. I could state my

preference for what I'd like to do, as the book suggests, but I'm at a loss for what else we would do besides grab a bite. I wouldn't mind going home, but I'm too chicken to pull the plug after only ten minutes. I go along with his plan to validate his masculinity in being the planner. We step into veggie-friendly Mark's Kitchen at the end of a long, noisy line packed with earth mothers pushing strollers and dads holding the Sunday *Times*. Everyone is wearing Crocs.

"I'd like the vegan plate, but can I get the potatoes instead of toast?" Yogadancer asks the waitress and then turns to me: "I've had my quotient of bread today." He smiles at me knowingly because we've already discussed the evils of wheat and dairy. "And I'd like to add the spinach tofu cakes and ditch the soysage."

"No problem." The waitress is leaning over, smiling and writing, the tip of her ponytail dangling over a chandelier earring and onto her pad.

"Actually, can I get fresh fruit instead of the potatoes?"

"We can do that, of course." She knows how to surrender.

"Is it really fresh? What kind of fruit is there?" He winks at me and I know my smile looks more constipated than agreeable.

"Cantaloupe, strawberries, and I think blueberries. I can check."

"Do you mind?" He turns back to me, almost sheepish. "Never hurts to ask." He's so calm and happy.

I'm annoyed by how high-maintenance his breakfast request is, and jealous because his meal sounds better than my two eggs with tofu and carrot/apple juice. I rarely ever consider manipulating menu items beyond asking for dressing on the side. Maybe I can learn something from Yogadancer about not being afraid to ask for what I want.

Instead, I learn all about his massage school client who ejaculated on his table.

"What?" Did I hear him right? Did he say "ejaculate"?

Yogadancer nods, frowning. "He took so long to get dressed and when he finally came out and went to the bathroom, I went in to pull up the sheets and saw that he'd ejaculated on them."

I wonder if the table two inches from us can hear. Of course they can hear. We're only two inches away.

He shakes his head and bites into the spinach tofu cake that I wish I had. "How's the carrot juice?"

The Goddess of Fun and Light finds the entertainment in her situation and focuses on that. I plunge my straw through the foamy orange head and nod brightly. "Good. And pretty to look at."

"So are your eyes." He's so earnest. It's sincere, but also forced and cheesy. I don't want this gift from him. But for practice, I take it without an ounce of self-flagellation.

"Thanks." I smile at him over the scramble of animal and non-animal products on my plate, trying to flirt but feeling nothing. I also feel nothing when he kisses me on the lips good-bye. It wasn't a bad kiss. He seems to be a good kisser, and with all the yoga-massage business, probably good in the sack, too. He's probably into tantric sex like Sting and can go for seventeen days straight. Alas, I was not interested in finding out for sure.

Later that week, I kiss Handshake Guy for the last time, too. The relationship wasn't something I wanted to pursue, though I wasn't sure why, since he did everything right. It would be easy to blame my uncertainty on the fact that he's not long for D.C. But I've never let that type of barrier stop me before.

When I got home after our final date, I skipped over the waiting cat who tried to escape through the door, and I went immediately to the books stacked in the middle of my apartment for advice. What was going on? I found my answer in *Be Your Own Dating Service,* Chapter 17: "Breaking up is hard to do." The number four reason to break up seemed to fit best: something's missing. "You may think your partner's a wonderful person, but . . . and it's that *but* that has you thinking about breaking up . . . Do you connect in all three ways: intellectually (sometimes), emotionally (eh), sexually (not really)?" Handshake guy is a great guy . . . but. He's a great kisser . . . but. There it is. But.

Red flags are red flags no matter who's flying them.

For someone who's always searching for meaning and signs to make sense of life, I am an expert at ignoring those things when I see fit. For instance, I start off the morning of the day that will end in my first date with Jeb by ignoring my gut. Everything about me said, "Don't go for a run." I never run in the morning, but I forced myself into my running shoes and out the door with the hopes that thirty minutes of low-intensity jogging would burn off the stubborn layer of winter flesh that was still hanging on my hips for dear life.

Instead, I get pummeled by a lawyer on a bike who seemed to be handing down justice from the surly bicycle gods who despise runners, or maybe from the gods of superficiality who decided I needed a lesson in vanity control. Or maybe it was the loving and benevolent gods warning me about what was to come. To be fair, it was I who made the illegal U-turn on the trail without looking and with my iPod on full blast. (Pat Benatar's "Heartbreaker" was playing, naturally.)

I think I caught the final "Move!" when The Counselor's handlebars pummeled into my left side and sent me flying and then skidding, elbow first, into the pavement.

"Are you okay? Oh my god. I'm so sorry." The Counselor has pulled himself and his bike off me and is hovering over my body, looking for life. I can't move or talk. All I can see are his clip-on bike shoes. The wind that was knocked out of me is replaced with shock, which slowly opens up to let in the searing pain.

I can feel gashed skin everywhere. I don't want to look at my hands or my elbow because I'm not sure bones aren't protruding from my arms.

Indeed, my elbow and forearm look like I brushed up against a sanding machine, the mounds of my palms have thick flaps of skin hanging from them, and my left ankle features a run of neatly spaced spoke holes below a dripping gash, compliments of The Counselor's pedal.

"I'm all right." I hobble up to standing.

"I was going way too fast. I'm so sorry. I have my cell phone. I can call someone for you."

And this is where I get sad. Here, in the city, I have no one to call for this type of thing. No boyfriend, no husband to take care of me when I need someone. Just my cat. I feel alone. Really alone.

The Counselor walks with me until I've convinced him I'm fine, and the second he cycles off, the tears well.

By the time I got a cab home, I was sobbing uncontrollably. "Mom." I cry into the phone. I hate making this call, because I will terrify my mother. She's always waiting for The Call. The there's-been-an-accident call. The call of catastrophe and doom.

"What's wrong? What happened?" Worry and fear consume her voice.

As soon as she knows I'm fine, that I don't need to go to the hospital, and promises to come to my apartment to take care of me, she asks the question I knew she would ask.

"So was he single?"

Even though I'm mad at her for asking and not continuing to feed into my sadness and pain, I know the answer to this because I looked at The Counselor's left hand and saw a flash of gold under his mesh bike gloves.

It didn't matter though, because I was meeting Jeb.

"We gotta hug because I can't shake hands." I hold up my bandaged palms for Jeb to see. I'd sat on a green bench staring up at the leaves in the trees above, thinking about how my life was going to change when Jeb crossed the bridge from the Metro station and into my life. The minute I saw him, the throbbing and stinging disappeared. I was smitten. He looked even better than

I imagined. The chemistry ran amok through my veins—and washed over me. A-*ha*.

We embrace awkwardly, absolutely not ready to be this close, but I didn't care. I wanted to jump into his lanky arms.

"It's like you have stigmata." He's bending over to inspect the damage and I check out his hair. I love his hair. I don't know why, but I like the fact that it's dark and straight and floppy.

I laugh and look down at the blood starting to soak through each of the bandages on my palms. Then he giggles. It's throaty and high. I'm taken. I want to grab his hand. I want everyone to know we're together. The stars are still invisible in the daylight, but I can feel them aligning.

"Where you wanna go?" He swings his messenger bag around to his opposite side so there's no obstruction between us.

"The Reef? Good roof deck, and it is so wonderful outside." I smile up at him and he grins his lopsided grin. Swoon.

"Sorry I was a little late. I had to get my hair cut." Jeb speaks slowly through a light Southern accent. We're sitting at the same table I sat at with Scrappy13 almost exactly a year ago. "You look great, by the way."

My cheeks flush. I look him right in the eye and accept his compliment with grace. I'd picked through every last item in my closet before settling on my new flowered top with cap sleeves and a hodgepodge of gauze products that are now gradually slipping off my wounds from nervous sweat.

Aside from graciously accepting compliments and keeping expectations in check, I had already decided not to use book advice for this date. It has to be me. Call it the control group.

Whatever. If this doesn't work out, I need it to be my fault, not because I manipulated the situation with silence or a hair flip. "I think your hair turned out great, too. Not that I know what it looked like before." This might have been the dumbest thing I've ever said. Maybe I *should* be following a book.

"Eh. It's kinda junked up back here." He reaches around and rubs the back of his crown.

I love that he cares about his hair, buys twenty-dollar pomade, and feels guilty driving to work because it's bad for the environment.

When he smiles at me with his gentle brown eyes, everything else in my visual field scuttles away. I can't even think about the menu and don't care that he's wearing brown houndstooth in the spring or that his bottom teeth lean left.

The waiter comes by three times before we order because we're talking so much.

He looks at me with his head cocked to the side and with crinkly eyes. I melt. He motions to his lip with his index finger. "You have something there." He looks down while my hand flies to my mouth to retrieve the errant bit that can't be food because I haven't started to eat. Is that a piece of lime? I don't have any lime in my beer. I wipe my finger on my napkin. Suspicions confirmed. It's a booger. Shit. He quietly pretends he doesn't see or notice, but I'm mortified. I bet it flew out of my nose and he watched it land right on my lip. I want to go to the bathroom to check for more potential green projectiles, but that seems too obvious.

I forge on. "How'd you end up in D.C.?"

He looks up at me from his croutons. "I followed a girl." He's sheepish.

The red flag begins its ascent. "Oh, okay." There's no need to get into this now on the first date, but I'm curious. "So how long have you been here?"

"I moved to Bethesda a few months ago." He picks at the croutons on his salad, but isn't really eating.

"Where were you living before?" I want the time line. I want to know exactly how long he hasn't been dating someone.

"In D.C., a couple miles away." His answers are clipped but I continue to dig.

"Oh, why'd you move?" I take a bite of my veggie burger and pretend to be calm even though I know what's coming.

"Because it didn't work out with the girl and we had to sell our place."

Red flags slap me across the face—left, then right, then upside the head.

He quickly adds that they broke up *amicably* six months ago. I smile in relief. I can work with this, but I need to know one more thing.

"So this is your first date since you broke up?" I put it out there as unthreatening as I can.

He falters. "Well, I've been talking to a psychiatrist online but I don't think I want to go out with her. She's a psychiatrist."

Not this. Why is he talking about someone else he's considering dating on a first date with me?

"I don't think I can help you with that." I smile, but I'm firm.

Warning flags obstruct my vision. It's like Christo and Jean-Claude set up their Central Park gates project on the Reef's roof deck, which has all of a sudden turned ten degrees cooler and windy. I'm freezing.

"Yeah, sorry. Are you cold? Do you want to borrow my jacket?"

"Thank you." I wrap his coat around my shoulders. It's huge and reminds me of wearing my high-school boyfriend's letter jacket. It feels good. I feel protected.

"So, log homes, huh? What's that all about?"

I deliver my usual speech and theoretically build a log home for him (and me). He laughs, but it's a conversation killer. Silence. If I were using the books I would have sat there waiting. But I'm not. I'm me. Stupid, lame me who comes up with stupid, lame date topics. "So, do you come to the Reef a lot, Jeb?"

"Has the conversation gone that bad?"

"Hmmm. How about your job? I have no idea what you do all day."

"It's okay. I'm actually looking for something else right now. It's not very challenging." He pops a crouton in his mouth. "I think we need a new topic." He hasn't touched his lettuce.

I reach into my bag of light date topics and pull out birthdays.

"Are you asking me my birthday so you can do the whole astrology thing on me?"

Yes. "No! I'm curious and changing the subject to something I can speak to because my birthday is coming up!"

But I do the whole astrology thing in my head, and we're not compatible. Cancer and Gemini. Not a good match. Screw horoscopes. Screw the flags. Screw the signs.

* * *

"Thanks for letting me borrow your coat." I hand back Jeb's jacket while we say good-bye on the same corner where we met. We're not doing the postdate shuffle. I'm rooted and waiting. My bandages are hanging by the last adhesive thread that miraculously didn't get saturated by the sweat piling in my palms from nerves. Are we going to kiss? Normally, I'd be rushing through the good-bye, not able to deal with my anxiety. Right now, I just want to kiss him because I have to know if he's a good kisser. When he goes in for a hug, it seems like he might kiss me, too, so I go ahead and make it happen.

"Oh. I get a kiss on the lips?" Jeb mumbles into my mouth. I guess he wasn't going to kiss me.

We kiss again, both of us with our eyes open. He pulls away and hugs me a little longer than necessary, leaning over to nuzzle my neck, and he kisses my collarbone.

I'm buzzing from head to toe. I want to keep kissing, but he has to catch his train. I watch him round the corner and I practically skip down the street, marveling at the blooming flowers and dewy leaves that have filled in the yards of all the row houses.

My phone rings three minutes later. It's Jeb.

"I didn't realize you were going to do that." He avoids saying "kiss."

"I didn't either."

"I felt like I was awkward. You caught me off guard. I can do much better than that." He's sincere and apologetic.

"I actually thought it was really nice. Sorry, I didn't mean to swoop in there."

"No, I liked it."

"I liked it, too."

"I'm glad we agree." We're giggling when we say good-bye.

The next morning, my eyes pop open at six thirty before the alarm. My first thought is Jeb. And his email is the first of the day:

> I'd like a do-over. That was the worst kiss of my life. I've only had two but, no matter.

He likes me! Then it dawns on me that I'm going to have to tell him about the experiment. I panic. I decide to put the conversation on hold. Anything could happen. Another biker could hit me, Jeb could find a job in Switzerland and move next week, a melting iceberg could flood the world. We make plans for our second date the following night even though there's a part of me that's saying I should take it slow. And Edie tells me to take it slow. And *Be Your Own Dating Service* says to allow several days between the first few visits, and Rule 13 says don't see him more than once or twice a week. But I don't care. The idea of Jeb has nudged out everything else. There's no room for *The Rules* or any other dating wisdom that would put a halt to the cathartic levels of chemistry I feel around him.

So when Jeb emails me on Friday to see me the next day (Rule 7 says don't accept a Saturday night date after Wednesday), I say yes and justify it with the fact that I will have a date right before with another friend of my my chiropractor. *Be Your Own Dating Service* says that the dating-around stage is much more effective when you actually date around with different men and have a few dates a week. "This gives you a sense of abundance and removes the desperation factor. You make better choices because you *have* more choices."

Actions speak louder than words—and poems.

"Why didn't he call?" I'm whining into the phone to Jeannine. It's Sunday morning. My date with Jeb never happened because he didn't call me until eight thirty Saturday night. He fell asleep. This is the weakest excuse in the whole entire book on dating. It screams "not interested!" Not interested in me and not even interested in making up an interesting excuse. I had enough common sense in me to know that this behavior was not okay, and I explained to Jeb that we could go out the following week as long as he called a day ahead of time to make the plan. Saying no to him was harder than I thought. Especially after my last date with the guy my chiropractor set me up with—the date that was supposed to make me feel like I had choices. Despite his glittery blue eyes, I could not get past the fact that he had a stash of squirrel meat in the freezer that he was saving until next hunting season when he could kill more for a proper squirrel stew. And his confidence was barely there. And we didn't seem to have any chemistry, which was a glaring vacancy compared to how I felt with Jeb, and it only made me want him more.

Did it bother me that I had to explain proper calling etiquette to a grown man? Yes. I hated having to be so pedantic about dating, though my therapy cohorts were proud of me for being definitive about my boundaries with Jeb. Personal win aside, the disappointment is a requiem ringing in my ear, and the little imaginary man at the little imaginary red-flag pole was working in earnest to keep from sailing his banner of doom.

Jeannine is much more forgiving. "It's weird behavior for sure, but too early to tell if there's a pattern of problems. You don't know what's going on in his life. Just see what happens." She's right. I didn't know what was going on his life. What I do know though is that he got my email long before he fell asleep and had plenty of time to call and make a plan.

I read about this in Atwood's book. Guys who come on hot and heavy and then pull back. Westbound Trains. No. It must be me. Maybe I was too forward, too eager. Maybe I do need to play hard-to-get games to keep men attracted to me. But I saw that Jeb took his profile down from the Onion, which would indicate that he's not looking for more dates, maybe because he met me. It doesn't add up. What does it all mean? I always say to my friends that he'll call if he's interested, which means if he *doesn't* call, he's not interested. But I'm not ready to accept this explanation. So I sit like a foie-gras duck in waiting, stuffed to the gills with the impending sting of rejection that's turning my insides into a bloated plate of mushy fat.

Jeb's crossed signals become even more confusing when I get his email on Monday.

Re: Ode to rachel
hi rachel

you're smart
you're pretty
you make me laugh
i like you

the end

I barely swoon because I'm getting pummeled by his inconsistent messages. He likes me enough to send me a poem, but not enough to make a date? He's directing traffic. One hand is telling me to stay back while the other beckons forward. I follow the one I want to see.

"What's this?" I trace the skinny white line on Jeb's scalp from the top of his ear to the top of his head. We're lying side by side on my couch, kissing and giggling after our perfect afternoon date. He showed up on my stoop bearing a pint of raspberries. "Nature's candy," he said. A peace offering. I tried not to look as excited as I was to see him. I'd quelled some of my anxiety about him with ten-dollar email therapy from Nancy Slotnick, author of *Turn Your Cablight On*, which requires a fifteen-hour-per-week commitment to dating. As someone who's put in more like twenty hours and is at the eleven-month mark, I don't have much use for the book. But I love the idea of email therapy. You get one question per order and she emails back within twenty-four hours. It's awesome.

I sent my 477-word scenario about how Jeb fell asleep and didn't call. I half expected the mail to get lost out in the ether. But Nancy herself wrote me back in twelve hours. Her email was friendly, personalized, and bullshit-free, like a big sister who's always honest. She confirms my suspicions that Jeb's terrified to get close to me. *He clearly likes you, but it is up in the air as to whether he is ready for a serious relationship.* She told me to go out with him if he does call and try to focus on having fun and not on the "relationship" part of things. *Don't hold hands—that's too couply. Keep things light so that he can get the impression that you are different from his ex and that a relationship can be fun. In short, be the cool chick.*

I'd been the cool chick all evening, blending flirtation with an invisible force field so as not to be too couply. By the end of dinner, my barrier was deteriorating and he broke through a weak spot in my resolve with a quick kiss on the walk home. So I invited him up to meet Bart, but really so we could make out. That seems to be what guys do, and I was certain that's what a cool chick would do, too.

"I had surgery." His answer is sheepish, and he defaults to his boyish voice that he saves for tough conversations. A voice I will come to know well.

I play with the hair around the scar. "For what?"

"I wasn't going to bring it up this soon . . ."

My stomach churns with anticipation.

"I have a brain tumor." I try to keep a square face even though my stomach is rapidly producing bile. "It's not cancerous. But it's grown back since my last surgery, so I'm taking chemotherapy to shrink it." He looks like he's expecting me to punch him. "I was going to tell you next week . . ."

"No, no, no. Of course. I'm sorry I jumped the gun . . ." I have no idea what to say. He hugs me. "But I'm healthy and it's not impacting my life. I just get tired from the drugs."

My mind is racing. I don't know what to think. And then I think about the experiment and am almost relieved that we both have these things that are potential deal breakers that we have to tell each other. If I accept his, he has to accept mine. What kind of reality am I living in, though, where squirrel stew (or bad hair or height or musical preference) can be a deal breaker but I barely blink an eye at a brain tumor?

Here's the thing: I have a close friend in a situation similar to Jeb's. I know the drill. And I know what I say to him if anyone he dates rejects him for it. I say, "She doesn't deserve you and she's a petty bitch." And I mean it. How can I possibly then become the same petty bitch? Especially when I have these feelings for Jeb—strong feelings that trump his imperfections. Nobody's perfect. Everyone has their thing. And just because I date someone who's physically fine now doesn't mean that in five or ten years he still will be. But the information weighs heavy on the fragile foundation we're still building.

Confidence, confidence, confidence. This was the common thread that ran through all of the dating books. Love yourself both inside and out, and know your worth. How you get to this point—that's where the books come in (and the gym and therapy and finding a new job) with tactics, approaches, and ideas meant to help you enjoy the journey and get the most out of dating. Some points are strikingly similar (make the first few dates short and sweet), some completely opposite (don't kiss on the first date, do kiss on the first date), and some totally bogus (rarely return his calls).

I don't know that any of the books dispensed inaccurate advice, per se. (For every woman comfortable with following *The Rules*, I'll bet there's a guy who loves that approach. Will they ever truly be happy? Who knows.) You have to be on board with what you're reading and believe in it for it to be useful. If you want to be the kind of person who plays hard to get, then be that person. If you're more comfortable being a Cool Chick, great. Whatever you do, own it.

And I firmly believe that when you meet the right person, all the rules and all the advice get thrown out the window. You don't need them anymore. They do, however, help you along with the process and perhaps help you get closer to The One. Or a one. (Even though I didn't think I thought of love so fatalistically, the term The One indicates a relatively fatalistic and close-minded approach. I mean, really, I only get one shot?)

Another common thread in the books: Honesty. First, be honest with yourself about what you want, and then be honest with your date about who you are—and, again, what you want. But with Jeb, I had no idea what to do. It would seem that I should have mentioned the experiment already. But I was afraid of the consequences. I was finally getting involved with someone I really liked, and even knowing the truth about him, I wanted to move forward. Though, technically, I can't. Not before I see the dating coach, who throws me straight out into the wild with the wildebeests.

Dating Coach

A Lesson in Confidence, Extroversion and the Art of Self-Promotion

"Man, this pineapple is *so* good. Hope you don't mind that I'm eating while we chat." Rex, my new dating coach, is starting off his day in Seattle, slurping on his breakfast during our first session. I'd called him from my desk during my lunch break.

Rex is in charge of training me, so to speak, and telling me exactly what to do and say when it comes to meeting men. I had many reasons for picking him but mostly I thought I'd be able to take tough-love lessons from him without griping, and he cracks me up with his fast-talking yet genuine shtick. We clicked immediately during our first phone conversation and I have a crush on him. Wouldn't it be so perfect if, at the end of my dating experiment, I fall in love with my coach?

Rex is also one of the most expensive dating coaches I found, but I got him to halve his typical one-month program, and for

$500 I get all the emailing I want for two weeks and two hours of phone time.

"No worries. I do it to my friends all the time." And I do. I'd stopped calling to catch up with friends on my way home because my commute had become the only time I didn't have to work, date, or otherwise be intellectually coherent. Now mealtime was talk time.

"Okay, so what are we doing today?" I hear him rummage around for his BlackBerry. "Lucy, get *down*. Such a funny dog. Okay, okay. Here we go." He scans the ten-page client profile I filled out about who I am, who I want to meet, who I'm attracted to, how other people respond to me, and what I want to get out of working with him. I sent him pictures of myself so he could see what he was working with, too. He'd told me I'd be an easy fix. "You're smart, sexy, outgoing, funny. You just need to put yourself out there." This made me like him even more.

I tell him about my day of watching how men responded to me, per his instructions. I'd put on a pink sundress, swung my wicker purse over my shoulder, and walked down to Dupont Circle at noon one day. "*Tssst* . . . Hola, mami," went the Salvadorian men clicking around in boot spurs in my neighborhood. I also got a "Haayy! Pretty in pink!" from a man leaning out his truck window, arm dangling down. No one noticed me in the Gayborhood (obviously), or at Baja Fresh south of the Circle.[15] There were

---

[15] I read on a blog that the best place to meet single men is in their natural habitat: cheap places. Chipotle was the example, but I figured Baja Fresh was close enough.

plenty of white-collar clones in line, but every time I smiled at one, I'd get a grimace back. Out on K Street, there were shifty-eyed glances from the suits and several shouts of "Hey, baby!" from the construction workers.

Rex laughs. "D.C." I can see him shaking his head with disdain. "D.C. is a weird town. I don't know . . . I find it really transient. You can't get a feel for it. You meet decent people but they're not embracing where they are."

Right on.

He continues to skim my profile, reading aloud in almost auction chant. "Okay, so you meet most of the people you date online and want to meet people in person . . . worried you might intimidate guys. No, no, ditch those guys online. You need a strong man; you're never gonna be satisfied with a wimp. We need to get you to widen the pool. Internet guys in general are weaker . . . there are a lot of angry people on the Internet. You have to know how to look for the hidden gems."

"How do you know?" I've been quietly typing, trying to absorb every ounce of wisdom Rex might drop from his beaker.

"Usually this means the men who don't go on and on in their profile and don't brutalize you with two weeks of emails before getting to the phone call. Get their phone number quickly and axe the people who you have no conversational chemistry with."

This is good advice, but I want to steer him off the Internet talk since I'm looking for his expertise on how to meet people *in person.*

"What do you have going on this week?"

"I'm going to a networking happy hour tomorrow." The last one of these parties I went to was a dud, but it's for people in my field, so I figure it's a good bet for meeting someone with like interests.

"Good, good. All you have to do with men is let them know you're open to talk with them. Are you going to the networking thing solo?"

"Yep."

"Okay. Here's what ya do: You walk in and scan the room . . . no looking at the floor. Just look around like you're looking for a friend and take your time. You want to establish yourself as *the* person to talk to. Walk over to the bar and use your cell phone as a prop. Pretend to text the person you're supposed to meet."

While I faux text and look around, Rex instructs me to target three men that I'm attracted to—the ones who intimidate me most. This is where I will fail. I've made it a habit to ignore these men, most recently the hot timber framer at the spring conference in Monterey. (Justin Timberframe was a no-show.) He wore flannel and had piercing eyes and a scruffy beard. He was also about twenty-three, and I used this as my excuse for why I shouldn't talk to him and instead entered the axe-throwing competition where I made it to the second round.

"Once you've got your men picked out, picture them as gigantic overactive Scooby-Doos, because that's what men are. They're dogs." Yes, indeed. But it occurs to me later that he doesn't mean dogs like I mean dogs. I thought Rex meant dogs, like assholes. He meant dogs like dogs—big dumb animals who react without much thought. To help me with this visualization, I'm supposed to download an image of Scooby-Doo to my phone so that I can look at Scooby first, which will make me smile, and when I look up at the guy I'm interested in, he'll see my natural smile and think I'm checking him out.

"You can look down and then look back at him and smile again. You can even walk by and make it known that you're available. No winking, though. If you're really gutsy, keep your cell phone in your hand, pretend to text your friend, and say something like, 'My friend is unbelievable; she's always late.'"

My reaction to this entire game plan is that it's stupid. But that is not something you tell your new coach. I will let him guide me because he knows what he's doing. I hope.

"I don't know if I can do this. I'm not good at talking to people like that. It feels so *contrived*."

Rex isn't interested in my can'ts. In true coach fashion, I get a pep talk about how I'm a strong, sexy woman, and have to make myself available tonight (and every night). "Call me tomorrow with what happens."

Maybe I can. I search Google images for a picture of Scooby-Doo.

Practice doesn't help if you mess with the game plan.

On the way down to Lounge 201 on Capitol Hill, where the party is, I practice smiling at people on the street with mixed results. Some smile, some ignore me, one girl liked my shirt. But when I get through the door, I choke. I detest going to these things alone. Let me say that while I've become much more comfortable and adept at dating, going at this thing of meeting men on my own without the crutch of a friend, website, or matchmaker is terrifying. And I've made keeping to myself an art form. I don't smile at or talk to strangers. And if someone talks to me, I unintentionally shut down the possibility of a conversation with awkward responses because I never know what to say off the cuff. Which is exactly why I've waited for the last possible moment to conduct this part of experiment.

Two rooms of people are already into second-martini swing. The loungy, hip-hop vibe feels incongruous for a Tuesday night. *I* feel incongruous. I'm the only ruffled bohemian in this sleek gray-and-black palette of tailored clothes.

Then I remember the texting. I stop in the center of the room and whip out my cell. There's Scooby. Oh wait. I'm supposed to first find the three men who intimidate me most and *then* look at Scooby before I look at the guys with an easy smile. Intimidating men are the good-looking ones, but there doesn't seem to be a lot of good-looking men here.

So I look for any inkling of intimidation and attraction. Beefy guy with dreads—nope. Balding fiftysomething with smoker's teeth—nope. The sallow-faced guy with beat-up loafers is kind of cute. He might have to do. And I like lanky, though he's bordering on slightly malnourished. But he has a nice way about him. I smile. He smiles back. Unfortunately, he's standing with a couple of other girls. This is unfortunate because, even though these women are most likely coworkers, they're attractive, and attractive women intimidate me even more than attractive men do. I don't know why. Maybe it's plain old competition.

The crowd shuffles and somehow I get pushed into a corner, muscled out of the mix by two cliques of professionals power lifting pink and green cocktails. The Scooby thing isn't working and I keep thinking how mortified I'd be if someone saw that I have a cartoon for a screen saver. I walk to the bar. Maybe it will be easier to talk to people there.

There's a cute guy to my left with his tie unbundled. I smile at him. He's preoccupied with ordering his drinks and doesn't notice. I take this as a sign that he's not interested.

I move into the front of the lounge, which is less crowded and easier to maneuver around. I survey the crowd and settle on the handsome, well-dressed guy standing alone. No conversation to cut in on or potential girlfriends to worry about.

I make a beeline to him, smiling. "Hi, I'm Rachel." Screw Scooby-Doo.

"Hey. Chuck Johnson." Blue eyes, skin like a cafe latte. And gay. So obviously gay.

It is just my style to pluck the one gay man out the crowd. But I'm practicing. Not every conversation needs to lead to a date, I remind myself. So I chat up Chuck, and meet Chuck's friend Keith, who's gay, too, and Keith's friend Lauren, one of those pretty blondes who's bouncy and outgoing yet not annoying. I'm doing this. I'm meeting people and talking to them on my own.

After Chuck & Co. take their leave (they're all going to the gym to work out), I return to the bar. Sallow Lanky Guy is still with his posse of gal pals, and even though he smiles at me, his stance is not open and welcoming. I balk. If Rex were here, he'd tell me to go up and introduce myself, since that seems to be what everyone is doing here. But I can't. I'm immobilized. Maybe if I try the brush by, he'll break away. I walk by and smile, making direct eye contact. Nothing. He does nothing. I *know* he's not gay. Not in those beat-up brown loafers. But there's no time to consider this any further. A huddle of three nametag-less silver foxes hone in on my chest, sounding out my company name. These aren't three men who intimidate me (they're more silver than fox), but they're definitely three men who want to talk to me, which almost qualifies. I'm swooped into their silver lair.

Once the requisite work talk is out of the way, SilverFox1, a burly guy with expensive glasses and even more expensive suit, still wants to talk log homes. SilverFox2 is vying to see what chance he still might have with me. And SilverFox3 knows he's outnumbered and is already off in the corner on his cell. Within ten minutes it's SilverFox1 and me, who might have a lead for me on a congressman's log home. I can't say no to this. I hand over my card.

I felt comfortable with him, probably a direct result of not being attracted to him and in direct violation of Rex's rule to talk to intimidating men. The crowd has thinned, the hosts have moved on to the raffle, and the party will be breaking up in no time. I recall a dating book snippet about not being afraid to move on when you know you're not interested. But then there was a part about giving everyone a chance and creating chemistry. Too much conflicting advice. I'm not *not* interested. (I have to stop thinking this way. Two negatives do not create a boyfriend.) But I'm definitely interested in Jeb, and that is who I'm thinking about and want to be with.

* * *

"I can't believe you didn't tell me it was a nametag event. Nametag events are so fun. I wish I'd known."

I'm on my lunch-break coaching session with Rex the next day. I feel like I've let him down. But even if I'd known it was a name-tag event, I'm 100 percent certain I would not have mentioned it to him, because who cares?

Rex slurps on his breakfast pineapple. "This pineapple is *really* good . . . Okay, nametags. Yeah, so I would've totally had you put a big question mark on your nametag or something like that to really call attention to yourself. You don't walk around like a regular nametag person. You wanna make it goofier, fun. Be different."

"Well, they were preprinted anyway." But even if they weren't and I'd known it was a nametag event and he told me to put a question mark on mine, I wouldn't have done it. It seems like something a guy would do. But this is why I've hired a man as a dating couch. To tell me what guys glom on to. I take notes.

"Hey, yeah, over here is the problem." Rex is talking to who-ever it was that rang his doorbell.

To me: "Hey, hold on a second. My guy is here."

To guy: "Yeah, over there in the kitchen."

To dog: "Hey, cutie! Yes, you're a good girl."

To me: "Okay, where were we?"

Rex's lack of focus is irritating, and I'm starting to wonder about his investment in my growth. I debrief him on getting stuck in the corner and on Sallow Lanky Guy and Gay Chuck.

"Oh. Well, you could have said something like, 'I can't believe you play for the other team.' Laugh and joke and make the most of every situation. Ask him, 'Do you have any straight friends like you?' Use every situation for networking. You never know who they might know."

I wasn't born with an opportunistic gene in my body. I have a hard enough time telling my friends I want them to set me up, let alone some random dude who I only assume is gay.

"So the text messaging thing didn't totally work for me."

Rex jumps in. "Oh, you gotta position yourself near the guys with that. Shake your head, make noise. Sell it."

To guy: "Hey! That was quick! Thanks for coming. So everything's all set then?"

To me: "Yeah, the idea is to use that same thirty-second story as your opener and tell it so many times you'll be relaxed and open, and the guy will be relaxed, too."

To dog: "Hello, my girl. You're so cute. Yes. You're so cute."

I keep thinking to myself that there usually aren't any men I want to try my story out on, and I keep coming up with all sorts of excuses why my coach's advice is bad. I'm resisting being pulled out of my comfort zone. I knew this was going to be the hardest part of the experiment, but I didn't know just how difficult.

"Talking to people creates energy. People are watching and waiting and getting ready to pounce, and will only pounce on good energy. What are you doing this weekend?"

"Rock climbing on Saturday. Maybe an art show on Friday."

Rex doesn't sound enthused about the rocks. "I want you to go out alone on Friday to the art show, wherever, and practice your story on as many men as possible so that it's second nature to you. Create a buzz, sell your story, practice it."

You know who has a good story? Kenneth. That night, we walk down to the Diner for takeout. He chatted up people during the entire ten-minute walk. We stopped and talked to Tammy at Safeway, he shook the hand of the guy who complimented Kenneth's "I Came On Eileen" tee, he accosted a girl walking by because he liked her dress and we bantered with her for so long, I thought maybe he knew her from somewhere. He didn't. Kenneth isn't afraid of talking to anyone. He dives right in, and people love it. And why wouldn't they? He's charming, he's complimentary, and he's really easy to talk to.

Two nights later, it was my turn. I stood alone at LeftBank's bar where the art show was being held, jugular exposed, watching, waiting, and doing not much of anything that Rex told me to do because it involved more Scooby-Doo screensavers, more picking out the most intimidating men and a shtick about how my friend was late because she wouldn't use valet parking, even though the bar didn't even offer it. Instead, I'd been hiding out in the back by the live painting demo, where I latched on to a couple of (female) artists and fielded one awkward encounter with El Rico, who was there on a date. Finally, at the bar, I got the number of a pretty Swede who'd been living in the area since January (he pronounced it "Yanuary") but would be moving back to Sweden soon.

And then I went salsa dancing alone, where I was immediately plucked up by a tall Peruvian man in tight jeans and cowboy boots, who was getting ready to leave the country to return to his homeland for the summer.

I wasn't discouraged by the transient nature of the evening's samples. I was so productive! Rex will be so proud. I got a phone number, I gave an email. I'm booming with confidence on my walk home. And excited for my date with Jeb the next day.

The window of opportunity for honesty closes quickly.

"I wonder what would happen if that branch fell right now." Jeb and I are lying on our backs in the park, quietly looking up into the maple canopy above us.

"Which one?"

"That one right there." I point again, wiggling my finger as if it had a laser pointer on the end. I drop my hand back on the nap of the picnic blanket, this time allowing my finger to hook around the cuff of Jeb's shorts.

We almost didn't make it to our picnic rendezvous, because, again, Jeb waited until the last minute to call. I'd already been out rock climbing, which yielded no men, unless you count the shirt-less climber who swaggered around the gym during his training circuit. By the time Jeb called at four p.m., I was so relieved to hear from him that I didn't set any boundaries by telling him it wasn't okay to email the idea of "doing something" a day before and then not follow up with anything until the last minute. We were still in that beginning dating stage when vague, noncommittal plans feel more like a problem rather than someone just being easygoing. But I squashed these feelings when I remembered the psychics' predictions from the previous fall while sitting on the couch waiting for my phone to ring. One said I would find someone very special this spring. Another said I would marry someone whose name has a *J* in it, is five to seven years older, and is not in D.C. but is north. Sure, she said New York or Boston, but she was guessing. Jeb is technically not in D.C. and does live a little north of me. The possibility that this could be he who was prophesized softened the steely shield that goes up around me whenever my idea of how life should unfold doesn't happen. So I whipped together a fabulous picnic meant to impress: gnocchi with pesto, tomato-and-cucumber salad, and a bar of dark chocolate, which I kept a surprise because I remembered reading in Jeb's profile that it's one of the things he loves.

"Where did you go for all of this stuff?"

"You know . . . around." I smile, secretive. I'm so pleased that he's pleased. "Okay. Sit up, close your eyes, and open your mouth."

I drop a square of chocolate in his mouth. He opens his eyes and I kiss him. He pulls me into his circle, where it's warm and safe. We've only known each other for two weeks, but it feels so comfortable and wonderful and right. This is it. This is what I've been waiting for.

A dreadlocked man wearing reigns of leather necklaces and carrying a steaming bowl of Tupperware in one hand and a stick of burning incense in the other approaches. "So in love, kissing in the park." His tone borders on menacing. "People in love need to be good to each other. People don't treat each other right anymore." He stops in front of an imaginary pulpit, keeping his physical distance, but still invading our moment. "Now, you two listen to me." He looks at us for recognition that we're listening and we nod our heads quickly, caught up in his bizarre scene.

"You promise me three things. You hear me? You don't cheat on each other." He stabs the air with his incense. "You don't call each other anything but your given names." Stabs again. "And you don't hit each other." He wields his incense as an "or else." I'm about to burst out laughing. Jeb tightens his hold around my shoulder.

"You hear me?"

"Yes, sir. Definitely. Thank you!"

He nods, grumbles, and marches away, followed by a trail of steam and smoke.

I fall back into Jeb. "What do you think he was having for dinner?"

"I don't know, but it looked good."

Later that night, back at my apartment, we peered through my picture window and over the rooftops across the alley to watch the night sky. Venus flickered at the tip of the crescent moon, while I leaned over Jeb's back, content. I considered telling him about the experiment right then. But I didn't. I convinced myself to wait until either he wants to talk about exclusivity or I'm finished with Rex. Whichever comes first.

Jeb beat me to the punch and suddenly asked me if I was writing about this—us. He said he had a feeling. But I know he Googled me. And why didn't he bring this up five hours ago?

I told him everything. As I watched him wince at the truth, I started to lie. It wasn't enough to express how I felt about him, that I hadn't felt this way in many, many years. I lied because I felt him slipping away. I told him I was done with the experiment and I wasn't dating anymore.

It worked. He came around. He said he understood.

I hugged him to make sure everything was okay and wondered how it would all work out.

I go over the lie with my family at my sister's birthday dinner the next night.

"What if I don't tell Jeb? We haven't been dating that long. We haven't said we are exclusive."

Everyone is more concerned with his reaction. It's the consensus at the table that the experiment isn't that big of a deal, and Jeb should be flattered that, of all the guys I've been out with, I like him.

I toss and turn that night, turning over in my head the same question I've been asked since the beginning of this project: "What happens if you meet someone?" I keep going back to my same response. "If he really gets me, he'll understand." I'm trapped. I want to be with Jeb, but I can't abandon the experiment this close to the end. And I don't want to.

"You have to tell him. Or you can be done with the experiment." Jeannine's answer is quick and definitive. There's no manipulating this situation. I have to put all my cards on the table and let the chips fall where they may. Intellectually, I know that by telling the truth, things will work out as they should, with or without Jeb. It's the same deal as when Jeb told me about his tumor, or when anyone else reveals the warts of their life to someone new. I have to give him a chance to decide if he can live with the situation. If he can't, then he's not for me. Honesty is the hardest skill to master.

I call Jeb the next night with resolve. I tell him I'm not done with research. That I have ten days left with Rex, that I have to continue to pick up guys, and that I will most definitely be going on more dates and not just with him. To my surprise, he says okay.

I spring out of bed the next morning happier and lighter than I've been in a long time. I'm joyous. Everything is falling into place. I got everything I wanted. Five hours later, my phone rings at work. It's Jeb. We don't ever call each other at work. The words "take a break" ring in my ears and snatch my breath away.

"I can't see you knowing you're dating other men." He wants to wait until I'm done with the experiment.

When we hang up, I cry at my desk. You don't take a ten-day break after dating someone for two weeks. I suppose it shouldn't have hurt as much as it did, because we'd only known each other for such a short time. And our relationship should have progressed slowly so that, as the warts of our lives were revealed and became deal breakers, a breakup wouldn't feel this monumental.

Why did he call me at work to do this? Does he not understand that I have to actually work now? It's so selfish and cowardly. More cowardly even than the way I break up with guys over email in the middle of the day.

I poll my advisory committee, though I'm not sure what about.

"Eh. He's a pantywaist. You don't want to date someone like that." Mike was glib and joking, but also protective. "He should be flattered and proud to date someone like you."

Edie and Donna wondered what his problem was.

Even Jeannine didn't get it, and she's always neutral in her compassion for both sides of every situation, never letting me get away with pat conclusions about the men I date.

No one seems to think the break is as big a deal as I do, though, and they all say that of course Jeb'll come around.

"So what'd you do this past weekend?" It's my next session with Rex and I would like to talk to him about Jeb, but I can't because I didn't tell him about the experiment, either.

"Oh, you know, I got a new mattress. Went on a coupla dates . . ." Rex tells me. He sounds unenthused to be talking to me. I get the feeling I've become a drag. Maybe I'm projecting because I feel like a drag. Maybe he can sense I'm not being truthful. Maybe he Googled me, too. I feel like such a cheat and a liar.

"How does a dating coach date anyway?"

"I do long dates. They're epic, sometimes four hours. Dates are trippy to me."

"What do you even talk about?" I'm dying to know how he runs the show. Rex has a good rap, though I can see it becoming exhausting after a couple hours.

"Half of the conversation is about sex . . . these girls are leaning into me, hair flipping, twisting their legs all around. It's amazing to watch it unfold."

"I thought you weren't supposed to talk about sex on the first date."

"Eh. I test the waters. I mean, if you don't want to *do* each other . . ." I agree, though his dating style would be included in a "what not to do" sidebar in every single book I read.

"Well, I didn't meet anyone I wanted to *do*, but I did meet a few guys on Friday night." I debrief Rex on the art show, sheepish that

I'm still not using Scooby-Doo or the text messaging method. I can't. I had to adapt to the circumstances. "But I did come up with a line that was situation-appropriate. 'Think you're gonna buy some art tonight?'" I expect Rex to be blown over by my ability to improvise his material, but he's not impressed. He asks about the Swede.

"He gave you his number?" Rex is incredulous.

"Yeah." My finger is twisted in the black phone cord. I was so proud of myself, because I'd used Rex's advice on how to give someone my number if they don't ask: "Easy. Lay a hint. Say, 'It was nice to hang out with you; maybe we'll run into each other sometime.' In other words, 'Helllooooo, dumb man!' Guys are bumbling idiots. You have to feed it to them."

I feel like I fumbled the ball, but I don't know why.

"You should have said 'Don't you want my number, too?' Better to bust him and have fun. Things like 'What? You're going to rely on me to call you?' Make him be a man."

He is equally unimpressed with my salsa dancing experiment. "Get out of those places. Go somewhere mellow and quiet where you can actually meet people and talk."

"Yeah. I guess I didn't really *pick* guys and approach them, either. They kinda all came to me. It's so *hard*, though. The texting thing doesn't really work for me." I might as well tell him I hate his coaching.

"You gotta learn not to care and put it out there. Be okay with it. The more opportunities you seize, the more comfortable with it you'll be. It becomes a game, and games are fun. You could be meeting six guys a week. That's three hundred guys a year."

Hearing these numbers makes me tired. No matter what I do, I will never, ever be able to handle that volume. I don't *want* to handle that volume.

On my penultimate call with Rex, he sounds frustrated by the fact that I didn't meet anyone at the coffeehouse during my jaunt there the other day.

"Go flirt at the fixings bar when they go get another cup of coffee. It's no different than a bar. People who go to a coffee shop to work are doing so because they *want* to talk to someone." Rex is out of breath because he's hiking up a steep hill. More than ever, it feels like I'm intruding on his time, mostly because he tells me he doesn't have much time today. And I'm annoyed that he's not completely engaged in my life.

"Sit across or next to them and start a conversation." His voice fades off into the atmosphere. "Lucy! Get over here, you silly dog!" Back to me. "Say something like, 'I'm so sick of my work; wanna do mine and I'll do yours?' Be interesting and funny, and act fast. The longer you wait, the harder it is. I'm probably going to lose you when I get up this hill, so call me back in fifteen minutes." I call back but there's no answer. Is he breaking up with me?

I email Jeb later.

> I don't know if I'm supposed to contact you, but I just wanted to tell you I'm thinking about you.

His email back was breezy and light. Maybe it was just a break and not that big of a deal.

Breaks are that big of a deal.

"This isn't gonna work." Jeb is sitting on my couch on Saturday evening a week later. His whispered announcement snuffs out the traces of wind that were still hissing in my sails from the last twelve months. I should have known it was coming. It had taken him a whole day to call me back after I left my triumphant message on Monday. "I'm done." I couldn't wait to say those words to him, especially after a disastrous date with a guy I'd picked up at a bar on my birthday. He sneezed when I walked by and I said, "Bless you." That was it. Jeannine and I had spent the evening concocting brilliant pickup lines and ideas on how to approach men at bars, and all it took was one natural exchange.

I should have left it at that, but I felt like I should follow through by going on a full-fledged date with The Sneezer, even though I knew there was no chance any relationship—friendship or dating—would form with him. I knew this because, after a few drinks on the night I met him, he went from benign conversationalist to obnoxious close-talker. That, and he was twenty-four. I was now thirty-four. I don't care what anyone says about how age is just a number. It's also a marker of where you are in your life and what you've learned from past experiences, which make up who you are. I know exactly where The Sneezer is in his life. He's working and hanging out with friends and getting drunk and close-chatting with girls at bars and going home and passing out on a beat-up couch that smells of puke and sweat. He wakes up every morning and hits the replay button. Three or four years later, he will realize he wants more. He will move, buy a new couch, and have more serious relationships. Then three years after that, he will be right about the place I am now, except at that point, I will be forty.

My brunch date with The Sneezer was terrible. We had nothing to talk about. I stuck it out for an hour, gave him a lifeless hug farewell, and the minute I turned the corner, called Jeb. He didn't pick up. And he didn't call me back for twenty-four hours. I was ready to end the break and he was nowhere to be found. I thought he would be as excited as I was and ready to spring back into action, but when we saw each other a few days later, the mood wasn't as light as it once was, and we argued over the experiment and the book that I would write about it. The Book had taken on epic proportions in Jeb's mind, perhaps purposely magnified into a convenient excuse not to date me.

"I don't want it to be Jeb and Rachel and The Book. I want it to be Jeb and Rachel." That's what he told me. I didn't have the heart to tell him he was the one turning our relationship into a threesome. Jeb also told me the real scoop on his last breakup, which he was still bitter about, wouldn't take any responsibility for, and was not in the least bit over. He had Westbound Train written all over him, and I felt it on our first date. I never should have ignored those red flags. I never should have ignored my gut. Even though Jeb started to come around by the time we said good night, things weren't as sweet as they were two weeks before.

I didn't want to see the breakup coming because, in my mind, it was all going to work out. I'd had lunch with my dad the day before and we dissected the whole issue. We rarely have heart-to-heart conversations, so when he speaks up, I listen. I told him I was thinking about leaving Jeb out of The Book. But I wasn't sure how I could do that and still do my story justice. "Just write it like you want to write it and see what happens." He saw that I was about to turn down a road of unhealthy appeasing that would set the stage for an uneven relationship, and I never stopped to think that I actually shouldn't have to make this choice. My dad did. "If it's meant to work out, it will work out." These words are excruciating to live by because there's nothing to control or manage with this way of thinking. You let life fall into place around you and then deal with it.

With Jeb's announcement that he doesn't want to continue dating me, I feel like life has heaved a burden the size of the state of Texas on my shoulders, and I drop down on the couch next to him. He looks at me with pity—the type of pity that tells me this isn't hurting him a bit. The type of pity that makes me feel like he never liked me at all.

"I know." I actually don't know that it won't work out, but I agree with him so I don't feel like such a jerk for being so clueless. My chin quivers.

"Don't cry. You're not a crier." He goes to hug me. I don't respond. It's an awkward, seated, one-sided tent hug. How does he know I'm not a crier? I've cried every single time he changed his fucking mind. It's not okay. It's okay. It's not okay. It's okay. It's not okay. Crying in my office, crying in bed. I'm always crying. We sit in silence, wondering what to do next. There's nothing to talk about. We barely know each other. We hardly dated.

"Can we stay in touch? I'd like to be your friend." He looks at me out of the corner of his eye.

"Why?"

"Because you're a cool chick. You make me laugh and I have fun with you. You have great style." He ticks off my attributes in his baby voice that was once so endearing, but is now grating on my exposed nerve endings. This is what he thinks about me? I'm funny and he likes my shoes? And anyway, those are *my* criteria. And if I'm so cool, why doesn't he want to date me?

"We can try." It's all I can muster. My rule is no friendship after the breakup. But the idea of not having any contact with Jeb makes me even sadder. And maybe he'll change his mind. These are dangerous thoughts, and if I were my friend listening to me, I'd tell me to tell Jeb that no, we can't be friends. But my judgment is cloudy and my head feels thick. I want him to leave so I can cry. And I do. For two days.

On the second day, I call for a free phone consultation with another dating coach, Dorothy. I found her online and I wanted to see what her approach is compared to Rex's, even though I have no intention of using her. And I wanted someone to talk to.

"You can't date a man who isn't happy in his job. Just like you can't date a woman who isn't happy with her weight."

I'd given Dorothy the dime tour of my dating history, including Jeb.

"He definitely sounds like he needs more time to heal from his past relationship. He's not feeling confident now, and you don't want to date someone like that. You can't. He's working on himself." Everything she said made so much sense.

Her coaching method is to identify fundamental requirements (nonnegotiables) and use them to make conversational questions that I would ask on first dates to weed out men who don't fit. She says you can identify whether a guy is datable in five minutes. For instance, with Jeb I could have said, "Tell me what you love about your work." Which would have immediately spotlighted the fact that he hates his work and is not good dating material, because according to Dorothy, "A man has to be settled and able to provide before he invites a woman into his life." Where was this woman three weeks ago? Still, even if I'd had this info going into a relationship with Jeb, I would have ignored it. I *saw* the problems, I *felt* my gut. I *chose* to move forward because I liked him and am apparently so desperate for a relationship, I talked myself into settling.

I don't know if her formula applies to everyone (though I would bet a hundred million dollars Dorothy thinks it does). It seems risky to generalize this when there are so many other nuances to a person aside from his career status. What if he's not happy in his job, but he's still moving forward and proactively trying to make a change? That seems like someone worth pursuing.

She also tells me that finding a potential partner has nothing to do with chemistry. And as for the people you feel chemistry with right off the bat: "That's a bad boy and not someone you need." Great. She's just sprayed my whole science project with a flamethrower and explosions are going off in every corner of the lab. Chemistry is the one thing I've been looking for this whole damn year. It was the Holy Grail. Any one of the men I dated would have been perfectly suitable boyfriends if chemistry hadn't been an issue. If she's right, what was the point of all of this?

Rex calls me on Monday to find out how I am. It was like getting an email from a guy who'd waited too long to get in touch after a date and was now making a sheepish attempt to make things right. Rex wants to wrap things up. This is reassuring. I thought our relationship was going to peter out like all the others. But Rex isn't like the other guys.

I ask Rex if he agrees with having a set of questions to ask a date to find out if they're viable.

"There are no certain questions. You have to use your gut instinct. It's about being perceptive."

"What about chemistry? I read somewhere you're not supposed to rely on that." Lies. All lies. But I didn't want to tell him I called another dating coach.

He laughs. "That's crazy."

I tell him about the painful date with The Sneezer.

"You shouldn't have gone out with him. You knew it in your gut. You don't need to get involved in the youth of America. The process is about being selective."

"Yeah . . ." I knew this, but it's tough to turn up the filter when it's been set to low for so long. And it was an obligatory date. I felt like I needed to go for the experiment, though in retrospect it went against my original rules of only going out with guys I was interested in. Somewhere along the way, I lost myself in the process. I was going on dates just to go. To get out there. To feel the thrill and excitement and sting and burn of overexposure. It was good practice, and I have the experience of dating without borders for the most part. But eventually, I do need to start being selective. It's okay to draw boundaries, and it's most effective to do this when you know who's out there. Now, I know.

"This plastic packaging is . . . [grunt] *impossible* to break through." There's a surge of rustling on the other end of the phone. "I don't know why they make packaging this way."

"What did you buy?" I don't care, but I don't know what else to say. I'm tired of his personal conversations on my time.

"Free iPod docking station. Got it from my friend. Jesus. How can you *not* cut your fingers on this thing? Sorry, I can't do two things at once. I'm a guy."

I'm impatient and want to wrap up our conversation. "So I'm seeing that this is something that I have to keep working on."

"It's a total work in progress. By going out and doing this every single day you'll keep getting better and better at it.

"You have to know how to flirt. Be comfortable with being aggressive and getting men to ask you out. And then you'll find a guy and he'll tell everyone how he asked you out but you'll know you got him to do it. Men are uncomplicated creatures." He grunts again as the docking station finally erupts out of its plastic womb. "You know what you're doing; you just have to keep using it."

A time to break old patterns.

"I'm not sure why you'd want to date someone in his situation." Judith looks directly at me when she speaks while the others in the room are staring into their laps or up at the ceiling. I've been waiting for her to say this to me ever since I mentioned the tumor and surprised that it has just come up now. I've gone over The Jeb Thing for the 157th time and am still questioning my ability to break out of a pattern of picking emotionally unavailable men, and I'm still wondering if being friends with Jeb is even something I should consider.

"Am I supposed to say, 'I have these incredible feelings for you but sorry, I don't think you're in a good place?'" She's quiet. I get the feeling the answer to this is "yes."

I can see what everyone else in the group can do to ease the confusion in their love life. But I don't have an answer for myself. I seem to be okay with dating people who will never be into me. Never once do I consider that if I, myself, weren't emotionally unavailable, I wouldn't pick people who were, too. The pattern I'm so concerned with perpetuating would break. Instead, I settle, and I know exactly when I'm doing it. Jeb told me on our first date that he was only six months out of a relationship that included a shared mortgage and talk of marriage. He told me that he was not happy in his job and not able to pursue what he really wanted to do right now. And then the medical issues. These were the signs, but I chose to ignore them and concentrate on the fact that we had found this amazing chemistry, which apparently isn't enough.

I do attempt to be friends with Jeb. The next night, I take the bus up to Silver Spring to see him. It's pouring rain and the bus wheels spray sheets of water ten feet high. I get soaked. We hang out at a bar talking about, of all things, the experiment. It's friendly but it's awkward, and when he drops me off at my apartment at midnight and speeds off before I even get to my stoop, not waiting to make sure I get inside safely, any strain of hope that maybe things might work out is silenced.

I believe with all my heart that the clichés are true, that we are our own best friends and best company, and that if you're not right for yourself it's impossible to be right for anyone. You are so lucky to have you. Don't lose sight of that. Even if Jeb is fucking stupid.

Nan emails me her muted pep talk, and like the conversation with Dorothy, it comes at exactly the time I need to hear it.

And The Psychic from Chicago calls me on a Friday night while I'm wandering around trying to figure out where to get dinner. We'd been in touch here and there since our Chicago date, and he usually called me whenever I happened to be thinking about him. "I was getting some serious Rachel vibes," he always says. Tonight, he has a prediction for me: "You're totally gonna meet someone."

I beat it down with my naysayer bat. "No. Absolutely not. I don't have time. I have so much to do. I can't focus on another person."

"Nope. You're totally going to have a fling this summer."

The way he says it makes me feel dirty. Like I'm not only going to have a fling, but it's going to be with a group of swingers and lots of dirty sex.

"There's no way." I'm adamant. "Even if I did meet someone, which I won't, I don't have time for that sort of thing." With the experiment over, it was time to write up my findings.

"Okaaay." The Psychic singsongs his disbelief.

Turns out he's right. Minus the dirty swinger part.

I started dating again a couple of weeks after Jeb. I wanted to be the one to move on first. It's a bad reason to date because it's desperate, and I ended up going out with men who never should have made it past even the lowest filter setting, including a guy who ate with his mouth open, spraying bread crumbs and arugula all over me and disappeared at the end of our date while I was in the bathroom.

Then there was James. James from the holiday party with Lorenzo. We found each other again on the Onion and went out a few times. I liked spending time with him, even though our chemistry seemed to hover at a six. But that was okay, because lots of chemistry is bad, so says Dorothy. But he also tended to invite one girlfriend or another out on every "date" we went on. He always asked if it was okay, and I always said yes because I liked his friends. But still. It was confusing.

Then I met someone else.

Simon.

Simon, who I'd first glimpsed on the Onion more than a year ago but never emailed because I figured he wouldn't like me. Simon, whom I've seen off and on around at neighborhood bars and secretly hoped would remember me from my profile online and ask me out. Simon, who, on our first date, after I told him about the experiment because that was my new policy lest anyone else decide he wasn't down with it, said, "How do *I* get to be in your book?"

We were at Toledo Lounge, a dark dive bar with a neon sign that casts a red glow on everything inside. I recognized him immediately when I walked in. He was sitting in a booth facing the door, white linen shirt tinged pink from the neon light and eyebrows raised in recognition. I wore my new flowered Target top that I'd bought that afternoon because I felt like I needed something new for this date. It was a big one after all. I'd finally approached one of the guys who intimidated me most and locked down a date, even if it was over email.

I almost spit out my beer. "You want to be in my book?"

"Yeeaaah." He draws out the word in his soggy British accent, saying it like it's the most obvious thing in the world. A smile relaxes the perpetual look of surprise on his face. He's not the aloof player I thought he'd be. I had no reason to feel so intimidated. *And* he's a genuine six foot two, so I'd let his slightly weak handshake slide. And the accent. And he wears seersucker in the summer. And he's a writer and editor, too.

I'm not overwhelmed by chemistry, per se—I'd give it a seven. Maybe seven and a half. But aside from first-date jitters, I'm comfortable with him, and the need to create a façade of being flawless has left the building. I don't chat incessantly, trying to be the perfect hostess, but not because a book told me I'm not supposed to. Rather, I don't have to. *He's* trying to impress *me*. Our conversation is reciprocal, and Simon holds up his end of the dating bargain. He's actually dated more than I have. For fun. I seem to have met my match. It's too good to be true. And it is.

Simon sets down his Guinness and is suddenly serious. "So I might be moving back to New York in a couple months."

I try not to look crestfallen, but my heart sinks leagues into my chest. I can feel the disappointment in my toes. Everybody leaves D.C.

"What do you mean by 'might'?" I can't tell if I sound inquisitive or desperate.

"Well, it depends on where I get a job. It's still up in the air, though."

The disappointment continues when he abruptly calls our date to a close at the end of our second round. We'd only been out for an hour and a half. I thought we were having fun. Maybe Simon subscribes to the short first-date rule. But guys never follow those rules. He's not interested. Inadequacy consumes me as I fake a bright smile.

"You wanna go back to my place and hang out?" Simon isn't in the least bit subtle as we walk out into the daylight that's sidling its way into nine p.m.

He *is* interested (in something). He was hurrying things along so he could lure me back to his apartment. I can't think of a single reason that would warrant me continuing our date, especially since he might be moving, and that falls into deal-breaker territory. Then again, "might move" also indicates that he might *not* move. And he's just so cute and tall and a little goofy.

There's no time to poll anyone—though I'm quite confident

if Rex were here, he'd be wearing an orange vest, blocking the crowd on the sidewalk, and waving us on to Simon's place. The Rules ladies would slap me across the face for even considering the notion. "Slut!" they'd shout at me. Nancy from *Cablight* would say it's fine as long as I go into it not expecting anything to come of the night. But that's assuming that I have sex with Simon, and I already know I won't. Not on the first date, especially one without dinner.

These thoughts swirl around in my head and I realize how tired I am of questioning and assessing every single move I make. I have a stockpile of information that's bursting out of my head and shooting a mile high, and trying to mine the data in just a few seconds to determine how I should respond is ridiculous. Should, should, should. I've spent way too much time should-ing on myself and it's squandering my *jouissance* with life. I need to strike out on my own. I reach for invisible scissors and cut the cord. It's time.

I smile to myself and I make up my mind. "Sure. Why not?"

So I go with him and we talk and continue our date and make out a little. And I go home a couple hours later.

And he calls me the next night.

"Hiiiiii." He draws out his greeting. He already sounds so familiar with me. I like that.

"Hiiiiii." I mimic him, trying to be cute.

We giggle.

"So I was going to follow that rule and wait three days to call but . . ."

"Well, *that* would've been silly. I'm glad you didn't." I'm sitting on my bed, looking in the mirror and smiling into the phone.

"I wanted to talk to you today."

"I wanted you to call today." It's so easy to tell him this.

We giggle again. I wait, even though I don't have to. He's on it.

"So what are you doing tonight?"

He wants to see me again.

Maybe The Psychic was right. Maybe I will meet someone. Maybe I already have.

CONCLUSION

'll spill the beans now. Simon and I did not work out. We dated for two months. It was easy to get involved with him because I knew he was leaving. The outcome was forecasted and I didn't have to worry about expectations not being met, and I thought for some reason that this made forming a relationship with him safe. I knew the plan. There was no uncertainty. I knew how this would end. So we held hands on the way to dinners and watched movies on the couch with the air conditioner on full blast. I met his friends and he met mine. It was a proper summer romance.

I was wrong about the expectations, though. When Simon moved, I was crushed anyway. And though we decided to stay friends and to visit each other, I didn't hear much from him in the first month after he left. I started dating immediately to distract myself, but I was only filling up the space he left behind. After a few weeks passed—I was in a yoga class, in cobra pose, to be exact—I had a moment of clarity about Simon. It dawned on me that we were not right for each other for many reasons, regardless of geography. I realized Simon leaving was a good thing because it freed me up to find someone who *is* right for me. I smiled with this understanding, and stood in mountain pose feeling stronger than ever. On cue, Simon came to town a couple weeks later and said he missed me and wanted to get back together. I partially knew it could never work out, but how do you ever know? So I shelved my rule about do-overs and joined Amtrak's frequent-traveler program.

We broke up for good two months later. He felt like it got too serious too fast. I felt like if we were really going to see if things could work out, we'd have to work at it. He was dealing with a new job. I had no intentions of moving to New York. Our timing was off and it was not meant to be.

In the past, I would have chalked this up as another failure, surrounded by flashing red emergency lights. But this time, I just let it be what it was. I made some very specific choices in order to be with Simon, and I opened up to our relationship in a way that I hadn't in a long time. Some very positive things came out of being with him.

And both times we broke up, I picked myself up and starting dating again. Perhaps too soon. Even though the last year felt a bit like a body-snatching invasion with the little alien sitting in my head behind my right eye, with the controls to my speech and motor functioning making me do things that I didn't want to do, dating had become a part of what I do when I'm single.

I started this experiment with one focus: how to meet men. I thought that was the only issue. But it wasn't that simple. It turned out the business of meeting the opposite sex was a fleeting battle in the midst of a blood-and-guts war as I worked on my neuroses and confidence, and how they were affecting my readiness and willingness to get involved with someone. The scary stuff.

My hypotheses were right. I met a lot of people. I found some chemistry. I spent a lot of money and I didn't meet The One (at least, not that I know of), which, as much as it was a hope I held on to dearly, wasn't my objective. And in a way, meeting someone was one of the last things I would have wanted to happen, because then I wouldn't get to be a cynic about love and relationships anymore, and I can't think of anything more annoying. (Of course, if I did meet someone, I would be writing that it was the most amazing thing in the world and I'd turn into one of those people who pats the hands of singletons and says, "It'll happen for you one day.")

This experiment became so much more than I intended, and it was the surprise findings that were the most telling. The one that completely rocked my world was that chemistry should *not* have been my main focus. But even after talking to Dorothy and listening to a CD seminar called "In Sync with the Opposite Sex," which touted the same idea that the pursuit of chemistry isn't the pursuit of happiness, I was still dubious. How can I ignore chemistry? And how do you know when there's too much chemistry?

So I called Alison Armstong, the CEO and founder of Pax Programs Inc., which produces the CD seminars, and asked her to explain herself. She laughed. She understood her idea was a tough sell. "It's usually by taking the chemistry road to its desolate end that women come around to this idea of thinking."

And it's not about lack of chemistry. "It's not the absence of all attraction, it's the presence of different kinds of attraction. Look for resonance—that you get bigger around him. That who you are is being received and amplified. Pay attention to who you like and who you like being around, but you're not in a hurry to jump their bones."

She also threw in a couple bonus tips, including the biggest mistakes women make: not being clear about why they're dating, which leads them to *only* look for chemistry. Also, women are unwilling to be attracted to a man when they worry about what people will say about him. They worry about being judged. Yep, that would be me.

And once I opened myself to the possibility of being with a real man beyond the intangible ideal that I'd concocted in my head, I started to learn. I learned to listen to myself. I learned that it's not my job alone to keep up the conversation on a date, and that men, in general, don't want me to. Also, I learned that being honest and upfront about my feelings and what I want from a relationship is always the best policy. It's one of the hardest things to master, but it always produces the best results. I learned to be patient, to let things unfold naturally, and that if I ever feel like I'm doing all the work, it usually means I am. And I learned once and for all that if a guy likes me *and* is in a position to have a relationship, he will call. Period.

A couple of weeks after I finished the experiment, I met a single woman my age who dated around a lot, too, but without all of the pomp and circumstance. Karen did it for fun because that's what single people do, and she loved it. (She even saved all of the online profiles of the guys she went out with for posterity.) There wasn't anything to decode, no neuroses to overcome. She may not have been quite as aggressive as I was, but she was out there. She was a natural and it made me feel silly for feeling the way I did about dating and even conducting this experiment. I wondered what was wrong with me that made dating so damn hard that I actually had to go out there and figure something out. But then I remembered the Pew Project and all those single people who aren't dating, and I wonder if maybe Karen is the lucky exception to the rule.

Toward the end of the experiment, I kept talking about how I couldn't wait to be done, but I don't feel like it ever ended. I simply got to the point with dating that Karen had found naturally. It's necessary and fun, and I *finally* found a cozy spot for it in my life. The pulling and tugging and whining from discomfort have ceased. Almost.

The dating landscape will continue to evolve as mind-sets shift to accommodate changing perceptions of relationships and marriage—and the Internet. But the hope for love and romance will prevail, and businesses will forge on with new marketing schemes to get singles together. As I finish this book, dating coaches and matchmakers are getting tons of press (some now with reality shows) and dating sites are promising even more scientifically proven methods to help you find the perfect match. Online dating assistants have emerged and they will write your profile and email with potential dates for you, and Internet Dating 2.0 is in full swing with virtual dating, where you don't ever have to leave the comfort of your couch to go on an actual date. (I can't fathom . . .)

For me, I've figured out the problem of how to meet men. Whenever I need to get out there, I go online to jump-start a new dating cycle. I've managed to alleviate first-date jitters, too, and readily admit that I'm a good date now. Practice was not always fun, but it made me agile at something I used to fumble over. The formula I've figured out: Stop being so damn picky and let go of the mental image of an ideal; talk to more strangers, because it builds confidence and helps you feel more connected; be open to every opportunity, and when you do meet someone you like, keep dating around. And there's the mother of all lessons—the one I'm still working on: follow your instincts and even if you're wrong about him (or her), you'll know better for the next time.

Oh, and always wear lip gloss and blush when you leave the house because, really, you never know.